E

The Story of a Modern Day Fairy Tale

Josh Bottomly

Telos Books
Oklahoma City

TELOS BOOKS
An imprint of Telos Books LLC
Published by Telos Books in 2024
First Edition

Copyright 2024 by Josh Bottomly
All Rights Reserved
Paperback ISBN: 979-8304166126
Hardcover ISBN: 979-8304166010
Cover Art by Meera Abuelshar
Drawings by Josh Bottomly
Printed in the United States of America

All rights reserved. No part of this book may be used or reproduced, stored in a retrieval system, or transmitted in any form or by any means, electronic, mechanical, photocopying, recording, scanning, or otherwise, without written permission from the publisher except in the case of brief quotations embodied in critical articles and reviews. Permission for wider usage of this material can be obtained through Telos Books by emailing permission@telosbooks.com.

For all the people who helped save me

Table of Contents

Advanced Praise 1

    Icebreaker 3

    A Word 6

    Origin Story 8

    A Simple Theme 11

    Quest|Archetype 14

    The Slant 18

    My Eu-ic Self 22

Eucatastrophe 24

    Are We There? 25

    Inconceivable 26

    Breakdown 27

    Easter—Part One 28

    When You Wake Up and Feel Like a Bug 31

    The Body and Brain—Part One 32

    The Inciting Incident 34

    Me and My Boss 36

    A Deal with Myself 40

    A Normal Day in the Life of My Depression 42

    A Conversation Across Time 45

    Yawping and Falling 48

    I Should Have Known 51

    Red Flags 53

- Akinetic Mutism 57
- Me and Emily Dickinson 59
- The Enigma of Depression 62
- Becoming Aware of My Depression 64
- Therapy 69
- My Therapist Helped Me Realize 73
- Post-Apocalyptic Doom...74
- Depression is [Fill in the Blank]..75
- Dark Light or Light Dark? 80
- Some Facts 83
- Some Facts about Suicide: 84
- Some Facts about Depression:..86
- Toxicified Men 88
- See-Saws and Dark Matter..93
- Green, Yellow, Red..97
- The Meeting 99
- The Call You're Never Prepared For 101
- Things I Never Thought I'd Say as a Teacher|Administrator 104
- The Covid Antidepressant...106
- Noö-Dynamics 107
- The Multiphrenic Self 111
- A Nebulous Omen..113
- Anxiety is [Fill in the Blank]...117
- The Hero's Journey—The Call to Adventure......................124
- The Hero's Journey—The Descent 129
- The Abyss 133

Things Depression Says To You In The Abyss......................134
The Exact Moment I Entered My Abyss 136
My Kryptonite..139
What An Unhealthy Enneagram 4 Says And Does 142
A Twitter Hunt...144
I Googled 146
It Gets Worse 148
Things My Oklahoma Brain Says During A Tornado Warning
....149
Name Death 150
Illusions 152
Bad Omen 154
Things Depression Says To An Enneagram 4 155
Reasons Why We Hide From Each Other 156
My Backseat Days 157

Eucatastrophe 159
Selah..160
Things That Helped Me During My Dark Days....................161
Breakdownbreakthrough...162
Holland, Michigan 163
The Body And Brain—Part Two 165
Hell..168
Help, Superman, Help! 170
Jesus At The Largo...173
This Bit Is Called "Blessed" 174
Magnificent Defeat 176

If You Can't Change Your Condition	178
The Brain Is The Body—Part Three	180
Things You Do As A 45-Year Old Depressive Living With Your Parents	182
A Conversation With My Son	184
July 4th	186
D-Town	189
Check In	192
Testing	193
Group Therapy	198
Belonging	201
Test Results Day	204
The 1 Percent Rule	208
Tough Love	212
Arts And Crafts And Steph Curry	215
Final Exam	223
Selah	228
Things I Gave Thanks For During The Dark Days	229
The Corkscrew Effect	230
Things To Avoid	233
Things To Embrace	235
How To Show Up For Someone	236
Telos And Logos	240
Reasons And Loves	244
Things I Can Do Again That I Never Thought I Would	250
What A Healthy Enneagram 4 Does	252

- Things I Give Myself Permission To Say Now (That I Didn't Before) 253
- The Hero's Journey—Homecoming 254
- Gifts 256
- The Gift Of Gratitude 257
- The Gift Of Prayer 260
- The Gift Of Presence 265
- The Gift Of Joy 268
- The Gift Of Bad Days 273
- The Gift Of Place 276
- Selah 277
- Things That Fill Me With Wow Again 278
- The Brain And Body—Part Four 279
- Fruit 282
- Existence And Paradox 284
- Remarkable Created Things: 287
- Chiaroscuro 290
- Practice Resurrection 292
- Anniversary Day 296
- Acknowledgement 300
  - About the Author 302

Advanced Praise

"Beautiful writing. A book for our times."
— Jonathan Martin, author of *How to Survive a Shipwreck*

"This heart-felt book is sure to speak to the depths of your humanity."
— Rachel Cannon, producer, entrepreneur, and actress on *Fresh Off the Boat* and *Mad Men*

"Mr. Bottomly was my English teacher in high school. Mr. Bottomly's love of stories inspired me to become a filmmaker. His memoir reflects his passionate belief—which is something he taught us in his class every day—in the power of language and story to transform our lives."
— Brent Ryan Green, filmmaker and producer on *Silence* and *Killers of the Flower Moon*

Owning our story can be hard but not nearly as difficult as spending our lives running from it …Only when we are brave enough to explore the darkness will we discover the infinite power of our light.

—Brene Brown

Icebreaker

As a high school teacher, during the first couple weeks of school, I like to use ice breakers to begin the process of building trust with my students. Activities and games always serve as an effective lubricant for human connection. "Blobs and Lines" is one such activity, and kids enjoy it—yes, even the older ones. On occasion, I pull out the Esther Perel card game *Where Should We Begin?*, a thoughtful gift from my wife, who tucked it into my Christmas stocking. My wife is a licensed therapist and loves to "gamify" ways we can deepen our relationship as a couple and as a family.

Perel's game asks questions like: *An important object I've lost*...or *I'm surprised I'm still alive after*... or *When did you know that you were no longer a child?* Answering these narrative-inducing questions can make kids a bit groan-y and eye roll-y—especially tenth graders—but these icebreakers work like Gorilla Glue.

(Here's a doodle of a black box.)

Which brings me to breaking the ice with you.
I want to share four things with you about me that will help you better understand the intentionality behind the title, content, and flow of this book.

- **I am an ideator**. I love to read, think about, discuss, and write about what poet Emily Dickinson called the "Flood Subjects." This book contains a mash-up of many ideas—from literature and philosophy to theology and psychology, with a handful from the burgeoning interdisciplinary field of neurotheology.

- **I am a teacher**. I love classrooms, desks, dry erase boards, the marker residue that collects under my fingernails, physical hard copies of books, and, most importantly, kids. My students will tell you I am notorious for drawing doodles to illustrate concepts. My mantra? *When in doubt, draw.* As a result, many chapters contain my doodles—simple word pictures to illustrate key ideas and themes.

- **I am a storyteller**. My granddad passed his love of storytelling onto me. He lived to be 97, spinning tales from his childhood on the Montana frontier to his fighter-pilot days in two great wars. His stories were original works of magical realism. If you have seen the movie *Big Fish* or

The Secret Life of Walter Mitty, or read *Cloudstreet* by Tim Winton or *One Hundred Years of Solitude* by Gabriel Garcia Marquez, you'll know what I mean. The magic in these stories involves the potent mix of nonfiction and fantasy. While my stories lean more toward intimate and gritty realism, I aspire to evoke the same wild, quixotic magic my granddad conjured.

- **I am a stand-up performer**. Well, not really. But if I won the Oklahoma lottery, I'd take a year off teaching and enroll in Second City or the Groundlings, even if I were the only fifty-something in the novice program. In the meantime, I've included a few stand-up bits in this book. I'm curious to see if you laugh, heckle, or walk out of the club.

Finally, as a middle aged man and a trauma survivor, I walk with a kind of epistemological limp. What little I know is rim-full of doubt, a natural consequence of having one's worldview knocked off its bloody axis.

So there you go. The ice is officially broken. Let's begin.

A Word

If we don't know each other, feel free to skip ahead to the next chapter.

If we do, here's a word.

Not long ago, I listened to a podcast interview with actor Jon Hamm. You may know him as Don Draper in *Mad Men* or Cyclone in *Top Gun: Maverick.* In his newest role on the FX show *Fargo* (season five), Hamm plays Roy Tillman, a constitutional sheriff, rancher preacher, and defender of the American gospel. At one point, the interviewer says, *Watching you in Fargo I gotta say: I didn't know you had this kind of character in your toolbox*! They both chuckle, and Hamm responds coyly, *I definitely go to a place in Roy's character I've never been before.*

This book is my Roy Tillman. I go to places I've never been before. I say things and share experiences that may make you uncomfortable or even offended. That's not my intention, but I wrote this book about the darkest period of my life for those who share similar struggles with mental illness.

When you are in a dark place, you don't want G-rated lies. You crave R-rated truths. There's only one zone you can tolerate in the quagmire: the bullshit free zone. This book draws its lifeblood unapologetically from that kind of confessional space, one I didn't fully understand or appreciate until I fell headfirst into the abyss. So. You've been warned. *Wink.*

Of note: I didn't set out three years ago to embark on a revenge tour. If it's true that hurt people hurt people, it's also true that healed people heal people. I write retrospectively from the latter place, aspiring not to use my pen as a *flamethrower* but as a *balm*.

A final caveat: the personal stories in this book reflect "my truth" in the sense that I tell the truth of how I experienced things. While I have tried to write with integrity and fidelity, I fully acknowledge that some characters in my stories may have experienced things differently. I imagine the full-orbed truth exists somewhere *in between* our different perspectives.

Now—let's embark, my friends.

Origin Story

Origin stories have always fascinated me—how Anikan Skywalker became Darth Vader, or how the Numernorians came to Middle-earth. As legend goes, C.S. Lewis once dreamed of a wardrobe, lamppost, and faun, which later became the seeds of the magical world of Narnia. Similarly, J.R.R.Tolkien, early in his career as an English teacher, once grabbed a blank piece of paper while grading exams and wrote, *In a hole in the ground lived a hobbit.* Recently, I watched the film *Air*, which tells the story of how Nike convinced Michael Jordan to sign with them over Adidas. In a last-ditch effort, George Rambling (played by Ben Affleck) and Sonny Vaccaro (played by Matt Damon) pitched the Nike Air Jordan 1 to Jordan and his mother. The shoe's design featured the Chicago Bulls' colors–red and black—with only 23% white, breaking the NBA rule requiring at least 51% white. Nike agreed to pay the $5,000 fine for every game Jordan wore the shoe. The clincher? Phil Knight signed off on a groundbreaking deal: Jordan would receive a percentage of every shoe sale. Today, Jordan earns $400 million annually from shoe sales alone. Savvy move, huh?

The origin story of this book, however, is less about corporate ingenuity and more about the fellowship of hobbits in my life. My *Samwise Gamgee* is Josh Banner, my closest friend. He and I met at camp when we were 13. Josh was from Illinois, and I was from

Colorado. Despite the distance, we stayed close friends through high school and college. After graduation, Josh joined me in Oklahoma where we taught together at two different schools. Eventually, he and his family moved to Michigan, but we've made it a habit of carving out time each summer to see each other. In June 2021, we met up in Chicago for a week and stayed at the flat of one of Josh's friends. Both of us brought writing projects to work on. Enough time and distance had passed for me to revisit the past trauma without reliving it. My therapist agreed, believing that writing could be a therapeutic exercise. So, in a coffee shop near downtown Millennium Park, while Josh worked on his doctoral project, I wrote a short non-fiction essay titled "An Educator's Journey: There and Back Again."

Fast forward to September 2023, I submitted a proposal to give a PechaKucha presentation at the National Association of Independent Schools (NAIS) annual conference. I restructured my Educator's Journey piece, retitling it "Moving Beyond the AP: A Quest Story of Eucatastrophe." A few weeks later, I received word from the NAIS proposal committee: my presentation had been selected from among 800 submissions. In March 2024, I delivered the PechaKucha presentation to educators from across the country in the Ferrara Theater in St. Louis, Missouri. Afterward, a friend said to me, *There's a book here.*

That spring, I began clacking away the first draft of this book—what Anne Lamott affectionately calls a "shitty first draft." My goal was to complete a less-shitty version and share it with a few dear friends for feedback by early summer. My students often groan when I quote Gertrude Stein, *Writing is rewriting*, but this past year, I've had to live those words. There's been no shortage of drafting loops!

I hope that the years of labor—pressing down words like crushed grapes and allowing time to work its natural process of fermentation—have culminated in a book that, at last, I can offer to you. It's the story of my journey from life, to death, to life-after-death, and finally, life-after-life-after-death.

A Simple Theme

We know more about string theory, dark matter, and wormholes in space than we do about our brains. The brain is the last and grandest biological frontier, more intricate than Japan's Fugaku—the supercomputer of all supercomputers. That's why our minds are both unique and deeply mysterious. They function in ways we can't fully comprehend. And they falter in ways we can't entirely understand.

While we share some common brain experiences, they're never exactly the same. Words like *depression* and *general anxiety disorder* are like motorcycle handles we can all grip, but the ride itself is experienced differently for each of us.

Depression wears many faces. It manifests differently for everyone, with pain felt in varied ways and degrees across the gray matter of our brains. To that end, if books had to perfectly replicate our personal experiences to have any value, the only books worth reading would be written by our own blood.

There's no "right" or "wrong" way to experience depression, panic attack, or suicidal ideation.

These things simply are. Pain, like Pilates, is not a competitive sport.

C.S. Lewis once wrote, *We read to know we are not alone.* I believe that to be truer now than ever. All good books—at least the ones worth their salt—are, in some way, about ourselves. When I've read stories of others who have weathered the storm and lived to see land again, I've found comfort. The stories have given me hope.

I am a shameless *The Lord of the Rings* nerd. My wife and son never miss an opportunity to poke fun at my hobbit-like quirks. Last summer, I took them on a tour of the deer trails behind Magdalen College at Oxford. As we walked, I regaled them with tales of how J.R.R. Tolkien and C.S. Lewis once strolled these same trails as friends, sharing early drafts of their great works of fiction.

They were over it in five minutes. Hot, sweaty, and ready for ice cream, they quickly tuned me out.

For fifteen years, I've taught a college-level seminar on *The Lord of the Rings*. As a precursor to our study, I like to draw my students' attention to a moment in *The Hobbit* that has always been my favorite.

In this scene, Bilbo, Gandalf, and the dwarves are pinned down by Goblins and Wargs. Their situation seems utterly hopeless. Suddenly, a great squadron of eagles, led by Gwaihir, breaks through the clouds and swoops in to rescue them from certain death.

"Look, Gandalf!" cried Bilbo. "The eagles are coming."

At the heart of this book is a simple theme:

Bad things happen.
Hold on.
The eagles are coming.

Quest|Archetype

I always begin my *The Lord of the Rings* seminar with the same question:

What do you know about the story of a quest?

For a moment, a pensive silence engulfs the room. Thoughts churn as my students process the question.

I turn to the whiteboard, pop the lid off my black dry-erase marker, and glance expectantly at my new hobbits, signaling that I'm ready to record their responses.

A young man in an Aviator Nation red polo is the first to speak.

"A quest involves a mission—some kind of outside call to immediate action."

I start sketching a doodle on the board.

Another voice chimes in, this time a female one.

"The mission often contains a goal or a task. Like an assignment."

More doodling.

"There's a journey, often dangerous, full of risk," someone adds.

I nod encouragingly.

"To reach one's goal, one must show courage in the face of some kind of obstacle or adversity," another student offers.

I nod again.

"And, usually, the goal includes some kind of object, a treasure—something precious, of great value, and worth the struggle."

I put down the black erase marker, rub the residue off my fingertips, and step aside to reveal my doodle masterpiece.

"You've nailed it," I say, beaming. "Now let me tell you a story."

When I was a kid, I had a little trick I pulled on an occassional Wednesday: I'd fake being sick. Wednesdays were the day my mom would drop us off at school and head to her best friend's house for a Mother's Day Out—usually shopping at TJ Maxx.

My mom's best friend's house was like the Taj Mahal of childhood for two reasons. First, they had *sweet cereal*. A pantry full of it. Lucky Charms, Fruit Loops, Coco Puffs— all banned substances at my house, as forbidden as anabolic steroids or cocaine. At home, we were limited to the "healthy" stuff: Cheerios, Kix, and shredded wheat (without frosting). Second, their basement housed a VCR and a copy of *The Neverending Story*, my favorite movie at the time.

So, on Wednesday, I'd go full Ferris Bueller—sticky palms and all—and it worked like a charm. Mom would drop me off at her friend's house, and I'd spend the day gleefully devouring half a box of sweet cereal while cheering on Atreyu and Falkor in their quest to defeat The Nothing and the wolf, Gmork.

Quest stories like *The Neverending Story* have a very simple narrative spine:

A character wants something and overcomes great odds to get it.

Let me say that again. Hint: write this down in your notes.

A character wants something and overcomes great odds to get it.

Some of the students scribble these words into their freshly minted composition books. Others stare out the window, clearly longing for just a little more summer.

I see the moment to segue into the concept of the archetype.

"The quest story," I explain, "is archetypal. Some stories have an arch over them—like the Gateway Arch in St. Louis—that stretches across all cultures, all generations, all of human evolution."

"We tell this kind of story over and over and over again, with the same plot arc, same themes, and same kind of characters, just dressed up in different costumes. The archetypal form is baked into our collective bones and our subconscious depths."

As the bell rings, I wrap up. "In our next lecture, we'll explore the concept of the slant in relation to the story of the quest."

"Good first day, everyone."

The Slant

In my second mini-lecture, I tell my students that the stories that stick with us are the ones with a slant. The slant represents the upward, valiant, heroic struggle.

"Think of your favorite book or movie," I say. "Look at the story's central plot, and you'll see the slant."

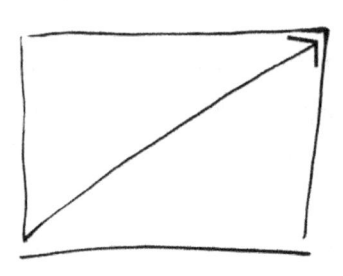

The Lord of the Rings is my favorite story—obviously! Spoiler alert: Two hobbits, Frodo and Sam, embark on a quest to save the Shire and Middle-earth from Sauron. To succeed, the plucky hobbits must battle orcs, cave trolls, black riders, a Balrog, a giant spider, a frog-like addict, and winged-dragons—not to mention resist valiant warriors and political stewards who succumb to the seductive power of the One Ring. Along the way, Frodo is stabbed by a Ringwraith's sword, pierced by Shelob's stinger, and loses his index finger to Gollum's fangs. But in the end, the One Ring is destroyed. Sauron is defeated. Good triumphs over evil. Epic, right?

What I've found is that the stories we love are ones with a slant, and it's the slant that we remember most. The slant is the glue that binds the narrative to our hearts.

The slant of *The Lord of the Rings* is profoundly shaped by a concept Tolkien coined: *eucatastrophe*—a Greek term meaning *good calamity*. This oxymoronic word describes how painful events can surprise us by leading us to better places.

I first encountered the idea of eucatastrophe in graduate school, during a course on *The Lord of the Rings*. In a 1936 lecture at St. Andrews on fairy tales, Tolkien explained the significance of eucatastrophe:

The consolation of fairy-stories, the joy of the happy ending; or more correctly of the good catastrophe, the sudden joyous turn (for there is no true end to any fairy-tale): this joy, which is one of the things which fairy-stories can produce supremely well, is not essentially escapist, nor fugitive. In its fairy-tale—or otherworld —setting, it is a sudden and miraculous grace: never to be counted on to recur. It does not deny the existence of dyscatastrophe, of sorrow and failure: the possibility of these is necessary to the joy of deliverance; it denies (in the face of much evidence, if you will) universal final defeat and in so far is evangelium, giving a fleeting glimpse of Joy, Joy beyond the walls of the world, poignant as grief.

For Tolkien, eucatastrophe was the deep magic at the heart of all fairy tales. As a Catholic, he saw it as the fairy tale at the heart of the gospel.

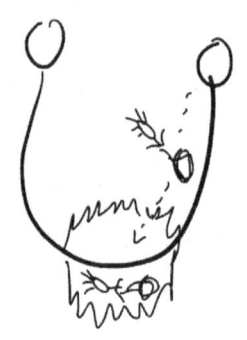

Eucatastrophe does not deny tragedy. Often, a sharp downturn occurs, unexpectedly, bringing devastating sadness. Gandalf falls in the mines of Moria, sacrificing his life to defeat the Balrog. Aslan suffers the curse-stab of the White Witch on the Stone Table.

Bad news seems to get both the first and last word.

But just when all hope appears lost, a deeper magic awakens. Something unlooked-for swoops in to bring rescue.

I explain to my students that Tolkien's message is this: while fairy tales acknowledge the *reality* of calamity, they do deny the *finality* of calamity.

Gandalf passes through time and space and is summoned back by Illuvatar to complete the quest and defeat Sauron. The golden-mane lion returns from the dead, splitting the Stone Table, breaking the White Witch's spell, and transforming winter into the spring.

Fairy tales—and the concept of eucatastrophe—proclaim that the last word is a good word, a *death-defeating roar*.

And with that, our second mini-lecture comes to an end.

My Eu-ic Self

I'm a few years removed now from the catastrophe parts of my story. That's another way of saying that I'm now writing from the *eu* space—the better place. There will be moments in this book where I will explore a conversation across time between my catastrophic self and my *eu-ic* self. It's my way of continuing the process to heal from the trauma. Neuroscience tells us that when we tell our stories of pain and trauma, we heal both hemispheres of our brain. Neurons refire. Cells repair. Synapsis re-web.

The world we live in today has a trauma shape to it. We carry around the darkness of our world in our bodies. It's easy for scales to grow over our eyes, blinding us to the light we can no longer see.

That's where storytelling comes in.

One way to make those scales fall is to tell each other our stories—not the Photoshopped versions curated for social media, but the confessional kind. Stories that traverse the full spectrum of the human experience—lizard brain fear, fingernail-gnawing anxiety, debilitating depression, antidepressant cocktails, *wtf* emojis, bluesy sadness, surprise birthdays, Michael Scott-worthy laughter, ugly-cry face crying, first kisses, first orgasms, first heartbreak, last days of school, snow cones, hemorrhoids, cataract surgeries, the thrill of victory, the agony of defeat, selfies with friends, dancing to a new Taylor Swift song from the vault, good coffee, good sex, good jazz, really good chocolate, road trips with girlfriends, family vacations to Wally World, the Niagara Falls, Buc-ees, a #1 or #2 from In-N-Out Burger, first jobs, getting fired, countdowns to retirement, hip replacements, watching the ball drop in Times Square on New Year's Eve, Will Ferrell in *Elf*, French toast, Sour Patch Gummies, secret love notes, boat rides at night when the Eiffel Tower is lit up, a mug of IPA beer, a glass of Merlot with a filet, and cliffhanger moments on the precipice—where eagles appear out out of nowhere, like grace.

Stories of *eucatastrophe* deserve a space in our collective consciousness, especially now. Because I believe that when we share stories of calamities, simply by telling them, we make something good out of the bad. At least, I hope so.

And maybe, just maybe, by telling our stories, we can become what Henri Nouwen calls *wounded healers*.

Eucatastrophe

"There's a storm coming, Mr. Wayne. You and your friends better batten down the hatches."
—Selina Kyle, The Dark Knight Rises

Are We There?

A single cell—that's how we *bigbang* our way into existence. Smaller than a speck of dust. Much smaller, in fact. Infinitesimal. Divide. Multiply. Expand and contract. Matter changes hands, atoms flow in and out, molecules form and pivot, proteins stitch together, mitochondria send out their oxidative dictates like emissaries.

We begin as a microscopic electrical swarm in an embryonic soup. The lungs, brain, bones, tissues, ligaments, heart. Forty weeks later, six trillion cells get crushed in the vise of our mother's birth canal, and we wolfhowl as we break through the magma of consciousness.

And we never stop howling.

Not until the death canal opens up, crushing us into its vise, scattering pieces of lung, brain, bone, tissue, ligament, and heart back into the galactic ether—where all is cold and dark and empty and silent.

Inconceivable

Three years ago, I was convinced I was going to die. If you would have told me that I would write a book about surviving my death march with depression, I would have pulled out a classic movie quote from the vault, and, like Viccini in *The Princess Bride,* exclaimed, *Inconceivable*!

There was simply no way I believed I'd still be here. Some days, I doubted I'd even make it to the next morning.

I had to lean on others to have faith for me.

My younger brother once texted me about a dream he had the night before. In the dream, I was flying. He believed his dream was a holy one, a divine sign of future flourishing. Whenever I felt like I was plummeting from the Empire State building, I would remember my brother's dream and pray to God that it would come true before I hit the 5th Avenue blacktop.

The idea that I would one day be well enough to write about my experience was beyond my comprehension. It was something I couldn't imagine—like angel's teeth.

Breakdown

that's where this story begins—don't they all, really?

Easter—Part One

April, 14 2019. Easter Sunday. That's the day I wanted to die.

I opened my eyes and couldn't move my legs or arms. Numb. Limp. It felt like a trillion tons of water had purled onto my face. My lungs burned as I breathed. Blinking away the film over my eyes, I tilted my head just enough to get my bearings.

A lava lamp the color of egg yolk bubbled and bursted. I exhaled.

I was in my son's room, in his twin-size bed, the one we got him a couple days after he climbed out of his crib in the middle of the night. He was ten now but still liked it when I slept next to him. I was like a big, human-size glow worm—the kind I slept with until I was five.

Okay eight.

Just a month earlier, I had a similar experience. I woke up gripped with panic, barely able to breathe, as though under water, unable to get out of bed. That time, I was in a hotel room in Miami on spring break with my family. Something had felt off the entire trip, like a vinyl record with a broken needle. Both my wife and son could feel it—the low discordant heavy note of depression humming in the background.

That particular morning just happened to be my twenty-year wedding anniversary. I spent most of the day in a fog, unable to celebrate the milestone with my bride.

The paralyzed-in-bed-thing was the start of something really, really wrong. I'd had days, like anyone, when I didn't want to get out of bed. But not like this.

A thought hung in the rear of my skull, near my neck, like a shadow I couldn't quite grasp. I didn't yet understand the strange physical effects depression and anxiety could create. All I knew was that I felt *winterdeath* creeping into my hollow bones.

I wasn't sure exactly what the sense of foreboding meant or looked like, but something hard and cold was marching toward me—like the White Walkers.

The past few months had been rough. So rough, in fact, that the only part of the day I looked forward to was the end of it. Bedtime had shifted from 11 p.m. to 10 p.m. to 9 p.m. At 8:30 p.m., I was taking melatonin to fast-track me into a state of unconscious oblivion.

The only time I wanted to be alive was when I wasn't conscious of the fact that I was alive.

When You Wake Up and Feel Like a Bug

Kafka had it right. Depression makes you feel bug-like.

You wake up and can't move your curved brown abdomen, domed so high that the bedspread barely stays put. You feel sluggish, unwilling to leave your bed. Eventually, you heave forward, banging your diaphanous wings against the bottom bedpost. You breathe heavily through your thorax as you drag your bloated belly into the bathroom.

You look at yourself in the mirror and don't recognize the scaly face and bulbous eyes staring back at you.

In your naivete, you don't think what you're experiencing is something anyone else has ever felt.

It feels so *otherly* is must be alien to the entire species.

But on the other hand, you don't recognize yourself—and you're convinced everyone sees it too.

They look at you and see something scary and alien, like a disgusting insect doomed to die in dead silence on a one-room apartment floor.

The Body and Brain—Part One

I've wrestled for quite a while with René Descartes's idea that the body and brain are separate entities. Hebrew philosopher Martin Buber referred to this split between the mind and body as an *I-It* construct. The *I* represents the immaterial mind, while the *It* represents the material body. In this ontological framework, the *It* is like a John Deere tractor, and the *I* is the operator inside, pulling the levers and driving the *It* around all day in a mechanistic way. This *I-It* binary often leads us to separate mental health from physical health—a division that can be profoundly misleading.

So much of what we experience with anxiety and depression manifests physically in the body.

Heart palpitations, back spasms, insomnia, throbbing limbs, clammy palms, and the buzzing sensation that often accompanies anxiety, for instance. Or the aching limbs and total-body fatigue that are sometimes hallmarks of depression.

Buber challenges this dualistic perspective. He argues that we've got it wrong. We are not *I-It* beings but *I-Thou* beings—fundamentally relational beings, not just with God, people, and our miniature schnauzer, but also within ourselves: mind, body, and spirit.

If this is true, then we are not souls trapped in bodies. Instead, we are *embodied souls*. We were made for integration, not separation.

Therefore, it's not "mind over matter," as the popular slogan goes. It's *mind inside matter*. It's not the brain and the body. It's the brain in the body.

The Inciting Incident

Hollywood screenwriting guru Robert McKee argues that every story of quest contains an inciting incident. Early on, something happens that jettisons the protagonist on a journey toward a new goal.

In *The Lord of the Rings*, Frodo discovers that the Black Riders are riding hellbent to the Shire in search of Sauron's One Ring, which has recently passed from Bilbo to him. Frodo can't stay in Bag End. He must leave his familiar hobbit hole immediately and blaze a trail—without Gandalf's assistance—into the unknown realms of Middle-earth.

In the spring 2017, I was in Austin, Texas, when I got a call from the Head of School. He asked me to consider a promotion: an opportunity to move into higher administration as the school's first-ever Associate Head of School for Academics.

I liked the sound of being a pioneer—always have—and really liked the nice new shiny title, for sheer vanity reasons. I was used to two-letter titles: *English Teacher, Basketball Coach, College Counselor*. Sexy-less. Way too George Castanza-ishy, right? Now I would have a six-letter title, long and distinguished sounding.

And then there was the money. Teachers don't get into education to make a lot of money, and I was no different. But with slow-creeping inflation and new expenses like braces, a 529 Plan, a teenager with an expensive palate for steak and sushi rolls, and a hypochondriac dog with monthly vet visits, my wife and I could use the salary bump.

In adoption training, one learns about the importance of redos with children from hard places, especially when parents make mistakes—which I've definitely had my fair share of as a dad. Redos can restore the connective tissue of trust and repair.

All these years later, I wish I could have had a redo with my Head of School. A chance to take the Delorean back in time, like Marty McFly.

Me and My Boss

People would tell me my boss and I were a great team. A dynamic duo. Like Kevin Durant and Russell Westbrook (with the OKC Thunder circa 2009-2012). Or Richard Hayden and Tommy Boy. Some days, we were. The *simpatico* was palatable, and our synergy reflected many shared values.

We had a lot in common. We both joined the school at nearly the same time. We were both competitive and liked to win. We both loved the school and its mission. Most importantly, we both loved kids.

But despite all that, most days I felt suspended in the liminal space between the poles of our dialectic personalities. Working for someone so acutely different from me was a constant source of low-humming psychic stress.

To give you a small profile of our differences:

Exhibit A

Boss	Me
Enneagram 6	Enneagram 4
Left-brain	Right-brain
Corporate background	Education background
Fortune 500	Not Fortune 500
Head	Heart
Allen Edmonds	Nike Jordans
Lexus	Honda
Numbers	Metaphors
Data	Stories
Measure	Experiment
Prove	Play
Measure twice then cut.	Cut then measure.
Live to work.	Work to live.
Iceman	Maverick

Exhibit B.

Here's a conversational slice from a typical meeting in the early years of our working relationship.

Boss: Good morning. How are you?
Me: Good. You?
Boss: Good. So where are we on teacher progress notes?
Me: Solid start, I think.
Boss: Have you generated a quantitative report?
Me: (*Google "quantitative" later.*) Oh. You can do that?
Boss: Yes. Blackbaud can run such reports and aggregate the data.

Me: Okay. So how often should I run a report?
Boss: That's for you to decide, but next time I ask, I expect you to give me a report by division.
Me: (*Nod head while scribbling note: "Run PN report every day!"*)

Boss: Okay. Where are we in the hiring process for each division?

Me: Good. We're honing in on a few candidates for each job opening.

Boss: Have you surveyed everyone for input about the candidates we've had on campus?

Me: Not yet. But I've had good follow-up conversations with a few colleagues.

Boss: Conversations are good. But I would also like to see actual data. So let's aim for next week to have a batch of data from a survey that allows us to review their thoughts together.

Me: Yessir.

Boss: Have you and the other division directors reached out to the candidates' references?

Me: Not yet. Getting there.

Boss: Okay, let's have that completed by our next meeting.

Me: Yessir.

Boss: Anything else on your end?

Me: Nosir.

Boss: Good. See you next week.

Can you feel the kinetically charged cable wires of tension?

A Deal with Myself

Here was the deal. My boss was doing what an effective Head of School does. Granted, he was fastidious, demanding, and, at times, hard to read in terms of what he wanted from me. He wouldn't deny it. But the truth was, my tasks, projects, and assignments were squarely within the scope of what someone in my position would do in the independent school world.

The problem? I was outside of my zone of experience and acumen.

Lesson plans, rubrics, assessments, pedagogical methods, student learning profiles, primacy/recency theory—those were my bread and butter. That was my tiny zone of competency. Now my world was overrun with reports, spreadsheets, budgets, management systems, hiring processes, and strategic school initiatives. Instead of carrying *The Blue Book of Grammar* in my backpack, I was lugging around a pocket-sized version of *Fierce Conversations*, flipping to the section on conflict resolution at regular intervals.

Suddenly, my reading list was packed with titles like Patrick Lenconi's *The Five Dysfunctions of a Team*, Brene Brown's *Dare to Lead*, and Tom Rath's *Strengths-Based Leadership*.

For my adult working life, I'd been an English teacher, college counselor, and basketball coach. I was used to teaching 50-60 students, counseling 30-40 seniors, and coaching 12-15 players. I could teach a student how to fix a comma splice, write a glowing recommendation letter, or chalk up on a winning last-second play on a clipboard. Those were all roles where I had the native intelligence, confidence, and experience to excel. Most importantly, I had the passion, energy, and enthusiasm for each set of tasks, challenges, and responsibilities.

Now, as the Associate Head of Academics, I had four direct reports under me, including a newly hired Curriculum Coordinator—a position I had I lobbied for to help with a vertical alignment project. Beyond my leadership team of five, I had 120+ faculty members under my purview.

I was out of my depth. I was drowning.

A Normal Day in the Life of My Depression

7:00 AM

Starbucks Worker: Hello, welcome back! How are you this morning?

Me: Fine. (Not fine.)

Starbucks Worker: Glad to hear it. Will you be having your usual?

Me: Yes, please. (Grande latte.)

8:00 AM

Boss: Good morning. Well, are you ready for another big week?

Me: Yes. The readiness is the all. (Lame Shakespeare line.)

Boss: Good. What's on your docket today?

Me: (As I look at my Google calendar.) Well, let's see. At 11:00 AM, I have a meeting with the division directors to discuss the fall exam calendar. (Shoot me Soprano-style.)

8:30 AM -10:55 AM

Sleep in the back of my Honda CRV car.

11:00 AM

Division Director: How are you?

Me: Fine. (Not fine). And you?

Division Director: Good. Did you have a chance to look over my proposal for adding teacher assistants per grade?

Me: I haven't yet. I'll read over it this week. (Or never and lie)

1:00 PM

Colleague: (at the coffee stand): How are you?

Me: Fine. (Not fine.)

Colleague: I always need an afternoon pick-me-up.

Me: Ah. Me too. (Something stronger, perhaps?)

2:30 PM

Student B: Hey Mr. B, we gettin' back our ICWs today?

Me: No. I haven't even started grading them. (I wonder if AI can grade papers yet.)

4:00 PM

Me: Hey, bud, how was your day? (Son slips his headphones off his ears.)

Son: Good. How was yours?

Me: Good, I guess. (Son slips back on his headphones. I turn on the sports radio station.)

4:30 PM

Me: Hey, babe. (Greeted by dog. Rub his ears.) How was your day?

Babe: Well, if you had called me, you would know that I had a crappy day.

Me: I'm sorry. Tell me now.

Babe: Too late.

6:00 PM - 9:00 PM

Silence my phone.

Dinner: takeout.

Walk the dog.

Shower.

Couch.

Show.

Bed.

The world takes on an amber tone.

For a brief moment, things soften the color brown like an old photograph.

I feel safe.

Then obliteration.

A Conversation Across Time

In *The Shawshank Redemption*, Ellis Boyd "Red" Redding, a convicted felon, played brilliantly by Morgan Freeman, goes before the parole board after forty years in prison. Red has had his parole revoked multiple times. This will be his final appeal. Resigned to the fact that he will never persuade the parole board, Red decides to drop the act and just tell it as it is.

There's not a day that goes by that I don't feel regret. Not because I'm in here, or because you think I should. I look back on the way I was then, a young, stupid kid who committed that terrible crime. I wanna talk to him. I wanna try to talk some sense to him—tell him the way things are. But I can't. That kid's long gone and this old man is all that's left. I gotta live with that.

At nineteen, I didn't really understand the gravitas of Red's address. Why would I? Thirty years later, I do. Like Red, I wanna talk to then me and tell him the way things are now. Talk some sense into him. I can't in real life, but in my mind, I have conversations all the time between now me and then me.

Now me: You need to think good and hard about taking that new position.
Then me: Why? What do I need to think about?

Now me: For starters, calculate how much of your work day you spend with kids.

Then me: You are using data? Come on. We talk in metaphors. Okay. Let's say 90% ish.

Now me: And the other 10%?

Then me: Colleagues, mostly. On occasion, a parent and a boss.

Now me: Now flip that 90-10% ratio. Ninety percent with adults, ten percent with kids. And of that ninety percent with adults, eighty percent will be spent meeting, managing, and putting out fires with adults. Sadly, some fires won't extinguish—they'll rage and roar until the whole forest is on fire.

Then me: And the other ten percent of that ninety percent?

Now me: Oh, that's the best time of your day. That's when you sweat bullets in meetings with your boss. You'll have lots of crucial conversations about how well—or poorly—you're running those meetings with adults and how effective your "crucial conversations" are going with them.

Then me: Interesting. A change, for sure. But I'm adaptable; that's one of my few superpowers. It won't be easy, and remember, the hard is what makes it great. (While making air quotes with my fingers.).

Now me: Did you just "Jimmy Dugan" me?

Then Me: I did.

Now Me: It's no joke, man.

Then me: Well, I don't believe you.

Now me: I know you don't. But you will. There is such a thing.

Then me: Such a thing as what?

Now me: Falling upward.

Yawping and Falling

The Latin word for vocation is *vocare*, which translates to call. There is a scene in the movie *Dead Poets Society* where Mr. Keating, played by Robin Williams, encourages a shy student to stand on his desk and yawp like Walt Whitman. One's yawp was meant to be a deep, primal cry for a life of reverberating significance. In college, I felt that scene in my bones. Teaching and yawping—that would be my calling. My vocation.

After watching that movie, I was so inspired that I changed majors, got my CDL bus license, and took a job at a local school as a substitute teacher and 9th-grade basketball coach. Eventually, I graduated with a degree in English Education and landed a job teaching 11th and 12th-grade English while coaching boys' varsity basketball. I had won the job lottery!

In a podcast interview, *Seinfeld* creator and executive producer Larry David once talked about how, as a new stand-up comedian fresh out of college, he would have gladly taken a deal to make

$200 a week performing in New York City nightclubs for the rest of his life. That's exactly how I felt at 22 years old, earning $19,500 a year as an educator. I was rich. Work didn't even feel like work.

Nothing made me feel more alive than inspiring young people to suck out all the marrow of life. I became my own version of Robin Williams' Mr. Keatings. I literally memorized and performed his famous scenes from the movie with my students. In the spring, while studying the Romantic poets, I'd take my students out on the soccer field and hand them lines from Keats, Wordsworth, Shelley, and other poets to read aloud before running up and taking a penalty kick, like they were Lionel Messi or Abby Wamback.

If that wasn't *Dead Poets Society* enough, it became a beloved tradition in my classroom to celebrate Yawp Day—a highly anticipated event where my students would stand on their desks and like Walt Whitman, sound their barbaric yawp across the rooftops of the world.

I was living my best life. I was living into my deepest calling. I was sucking the marrow of my own life.

In education, the only way "up" is into administration. That's a shame, really. Most good teachers are good teachers because they connect with kids. Administration is an entirely different job, requiring a different skill set. It's mostly meetings with adults about kids and rarely with kids themselves.

I didn't fully understand what awaited me in the administrative realm until I got up there. The sad truth was that my ascent into administration paradoxically led to my descent. Now me was right.

Damn. I was falling upward.

It wasn't until I ended up in an outpatient treatment center in Dallas, Texas that I realized the deep, dark depression I was experiencing stemmed largely from losing my yawp. In going yawp-less, I had lost any and all semblance of myself. I was completely alien to who I once was, like Alf.

I Should Have Known

Looking back, I should have known. It had loomed like a cloud—a cloud that would eventually break and rain down on me.

At the time, I was working two school administrative jobs: Associate Head of Academics and interim Middle Division (MD) director. The prior MD director had been at the school for twenty-one years. She was an institutional force—and legend. The school needed a stop-gap solution, a stand-in interim director, someone from within the institution to fill the role for a year while they conducted a national search for her replacement. I was the least qualified person for the job but the absolute perfect punching bag for parents in carpool.

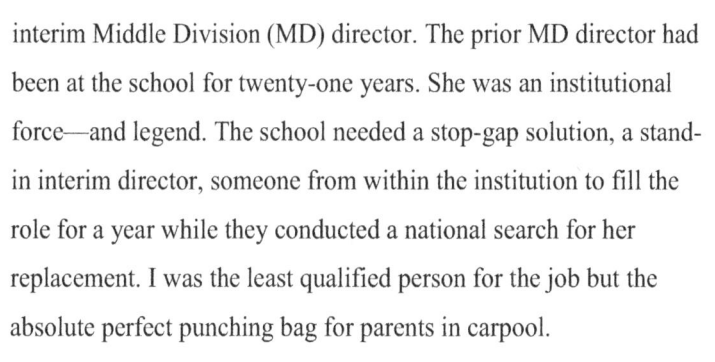

I once heard the story of a prior MD Director at my school who hated his job so much that some mornings, he would drive his car through the campus roundabout ten times—loop after loop—before finally exciting the campus. That story used to make me laugh. Now, it made me want to cry. Some days, I would sneak off to my car, close my eyes, and imagine myself in a happy place, like Happy Gilmore.

Everything radiated tension, as if my life had been built upon the skin of a balloon, with someone inflating it to the point of bursting.

Full disclosure: Middle school kids will take you to your knees. If you have been a middle schooler—or raised one—you know what I'm talking about.

Also: Middle school parents will take you somewhere far darker, like Dexter dark.

Red Flags

Red flags are warning signs. Sometimes, they don't flap high in the air; they're buried under the dirt, hidden and invisible. That makes seeing depression especially hard to detect, particularly for those who have never wrestled with the dragon. Their lack of experience makes it difficult to spot the dark scales beneath the surface.

Depression is an illness. But it's not something you can hear, like a congested cough, or see, like a rash of small bumps. Even though it's a serious illness affecting 280 million people annually, moving unnoticed among the crowd like agents in *The Matrix*.

That said, there are identifiable red flags to watch for among the people in your relational ecosystem.

- **Low energy**: Constant fatigue, heavy sighs, and frequent yawning without any obvious cause. (Except, perhaps, during my lectures on the Renaissance Period and William Shakespeare—those would elicit a normal response.)

- **Feeling blue**: Once called melancholy, this state can show physical signs, such as irritability, difficulty concentrating, or a tendency to make doomsday-like declarations. (This is just about everyone on Monday mornings or the day after the presidential election.)

- **Low self-esteem**: This one can be tricky to spot, like a hermit crab buried in the sand. Most people aren't comfortable talking about their feelings, and low self-esteem isn't exactly Instagram material in today's narcissistic social media culture.

- **Loss of appetite**: Or, sometimes, the opposite. That's what I experienced—a ravenous appetite, especially around 10 p.m., for a bowl of Apple Jacks.

- **Frequent crying**: Like when you can't find matching socks, or the ripe avocado in the grocery store is overripe. Or when you get the wrong Starbucks order—or someone in the minivan ahead of you at Starbucks pays for your drink. Or your partner ghosts you and doesn't text you back in five minutes. Or you watch a TikTok of two elderly people swinging on a front porch, singing love songs in harmonies perfected over fifty years of marriage. (That last one may just be a healthy cry, though.)

- **Anger outburst**: To be fair, this might just mean you're human—especially if you have kids, drive often in traffic, or have an ornery, entitled dog.

- **Anhedonia**: I first encountered this term in the film *Garden State*, written and directed by Zach Braff. In the movie, Braff's character, Andrew Largeman, is a depressed, heavily medicated twenty-something trying to navigate life. There's a scene where he sits apathetically on a coach at a party while everyone else dances, plays drinking games, and gets high. That's the essence of anhedonia—the inability to experience pleasure. The libido goes limp. The pleasure center shuts down. You can't enjoy a waffle, a sunrise, a Beyonce song, or Amy Poehler in *Parks and Recreation*.

- **Sudden isolation**: As an introvert, this red flag is hard for me to identify. Healthy alone time and unhealthy withdrawal can look similar. But if someone you know becomes quieter, pulling inward like a conch shell, they might be struggling with depression. There were times I retreated so far into myself that I couldn't speak or text. I had nothing to say because it felt like I was living on Mars while everyone else was living on Earth, speaking a language I no longer understood.

Akinetic Mutism

Some days, I stayed bed-bound until my dog nudged my arm, reminding me to feed him. On other days, I snuck back home when I knew my wife was at work and crawled under the covers again.

On those days, I always felt disappointed when I woke up to find I was still breathing. There was no relief. I didn't want to be alive. No—that's not entirely accurate. Death terrified me. What I wanted was more of a waking coma, a kind of upright, bipedal vegetative state.

I had recently learned about akinetic mutism, a rare brain condition caused by damage to the anterior cingulate region. It sounded like the perfect, imperfect alternative to death. With akinetic mutism, I could still track motion with my eyes and change positions occasionally, but nothing more. The ability to move would remain, but the motivation would vanish—like Bartleby the scrivener at the very end.

St. Bede once compared human consciousness to a sparrow flying in from the cold, lingering briefly in the warmth of a room, then disappearing back into the darkness.

- We are unconscious before we exist.
- Then conscious for a while.
- Then unconscious again after we die.

I wished someone would put a shotgun shell through my sparrow.

Me and Emily Dickinson

The gnarley thing about the mind is this: You can have the most feverish, chaotic storm raging inside, and no one else can see it. The mind is not a translucent window that allows people to peer inside from the sidewalk. It's opaque, like a thick curtain.

To the world, you might appear fine. Maybe your pupils might dilate, or your voice sounds a bit sloshy, or your skin glistens with a sheen of sweat. But those are just small hints. No one can truly know what you're feeling, no one can sympathize with the hell you are living through, or understand why deathsleep seems like such a lucid, rational idea.

To others, depression often seems like nothing at all—a trivial inconvenience, like spring allergies or a passing cold. You're walking around with your head in a thundercloud, but no one else hears the booming thunder. This lack of understanding is why the stigma surrounding depression persists.

And stigma? It's particularly cruel for those with depression because the stigma affects thoughts, and depression is a disease of thoughts.

When you're depressed, you feel like Emily Dickinson—alone in your room, staring out the window at the normal, well-adjusted people below. Nobody outside can relate to what you're thinking or feeling. You're terrified of appearing crazy, so you internalize the madness. You convince yourself that saying anything will alienate you further.

That's a shame because we know that speaking about depression helps. It's one of the few ways to break the stigma. Words—whether spoken or written—are the connective tissues that bind us to each other and the world. Sharing our struggles gives us a lifeline, a way to bridge the gap between isolation and understanding.

As humans, our natural East of Eden impulse is to hide behind the bushes of shame. We sew fig leaves together—metaphorically speaking—to cover our vulnerabilities. Then, we strut through life in designer Gucci figs, pretending everything is fine. But it's not.

And the only way we make things better—the only way back West of Eden—is to summon the courage to tell the truth. Not just any truth, but the whole, raw, wolf-howling truth. Only then can we rediscover a place of light, wholeness, and self-acceptance—a kind of prelapsarian innocence.

The Enigma of Depression

Depression is hard to understand because it doesn't look one specific way or have a singular cause.

At its best, depression merely clouds happiness, making it fleeting and temporary. At its worst, it casts a long shadow that follows you everywhere. It feels like bats are living in your chest, and the mind becomes a black hole—a tormentor spinning endlessly through the void of intergalactic space.

Depression can be caused by any number of possible existential situations.

- The loss of a loved one or a rejection.
- Mercurial weather.
- Getting laid off.
- Stepping on the scale.
- Seeing your scabrous-colored face in the bathroom mirror.
- Watching a presidential debate.
- An unexpected pregnancy.
- A painful divorce or broken friendship.
- A miscarriage.
- Seeing your childhood home bulldozed into a strip mall parking lot.

This is why depression spares no one. It can afflict:

- Billionaires with a chateau in Switzerland.
- World-class athletes.
- People with good teeth.
- Amorously happy newlyweds.
- People who have just landed their dream job at Google.
- Those who can moonwalk, juggle, and play Clapton's Tears in Heaven.
- People with perfectly clear skin and flawless social media lives.

It affects anyone and everyone.

The truth is, depression is an unseen, mysterious force. It's an enigma, even to those who endure it.

Becoming Aware of My Depression

Easter was a beginning–the first time I felt any kind of acute depression. Up until that point, I had no real understanding or awareness of what depression truly was. I knew my aunt had struggled with mental illness and had taken her own life after a brave battle. I also knew of a great-uncle on my dad's side who battled alcoholism and, like my aunt, took his life. Growing up, I was never made aware of my dad or mom struggling with depression. Years later, I learned that my mom had a bout with postpartum depression when my youngest brother was born. I was seven at the time, so I don't remember her quiet war.

In college, however, I vividly remember when my dad had a mild stroke during a wedding ceremony. He slurred his way through the vows and had to be escorted off stage. No one saw it coming. Only later did I learn that his ischemic attack had been caused by a prolonged period of intense stress, anxiety, and ever-expanding silent depression.

While there was somewhat of a family history of mental illness, it hadn't been a history I thought about much—especially growing up.

That was until the day I wanted to die at age forty-five.

That's when mental illness stepped onto center stage, like Hamilton.

Easter—Part Two

On Easter, I normally wake up and join my wife and son in the kitchen. We drink coffee and watch our son pop open plastic eggs to pull out jelly beans and dollar bills. Not this year. Instead, my son opened his Easter basket with only his mom. I could hear my wife's voice. She was overcompensating for my absence, doing her best to distract our son from the fact that his dad was still in bed. Eventually, my wife and son left the house and headed over to her parents' house for an Easter brunch. In a desperate attempt to send up a flare into the sky above the human wreckage, my wife called my Dad—something she rarely did.

This is funny. Funny because it's Easter—the zenith day in the Christian tradition—when people all over the world show up to church dressed in their Sunday best, all smiles with Hershey's chocolate stuck to their teeth, saying things like, "He is risen," "He has risen indeed." The irony is just so damn hilarious. It's a dark comedy. Cohen brothers-like. Or Flannery O' Connor. Here I am, on Resurrection Day, hope day, death-defeated day, and all I want to do is die. *Fuck* resurrection. Leave me in the tomb.

I heard Dad's voice from under the bed covers. I thought I was dreaming. In a good dream, Dad would pull back the sheet, tousle my hair, and tell me everything was going to be okay, like he did when I was a child. "The thunder won't hurt you, Josh. The house won't blow away, buddy. The storm will pass, so hang in there just a little bit longer."

Dad went and got me a glass of water. He got me to sit up, take a forced drink, and eventually move into the living room. Sinking into the couch, I grabbed a blanket and draped it over my shoulders. For a while, I stared silently at a dirt stain on the taupe-colored couch. The dog must have dragged it in from the backyard, probably on a rainy day last week. Dad asked me what I was feeling. I didn't really know. Nothing, if I was honest. It was more a sense of what I'd become—some cheap cocktail of dead skin cells and hollow particles floating in the forlorn air.

All I wanted to do was join Robert Frost in the dark snow-covered woods of oblivion. But I couldn't. I had many miles yet to go. I had loved ones who depended on me. Deathsleep was not an option. So I opened my eyes and tried to form words. They didn't come at first, but then something in the subterranean depths roiled through the dark dirt soils and geysered up out of me: "I just don't know what to do!" Next thing I know, I sounded like a wounded, dying wolf.

Dad came over, put his arm around me, and let my shoulders heave and convulse into his chest until all the pent-up exhaustion had turned into snot and wet, greenish smear stains on his nicely ironed pink Oxford shirt.

Eventually, my wolfhowling stopped and all went silent. Like the silence that settles over dark waters after the storm has passed.

Frederick Beuchner once wrote, *Pay attention to the things that bring a tear to your eye or a lump to your throat because they are signs that the holy is drawing near.*

I'm not sure Beuchner had in mind what I unleashed on Dad. It's hard to believe that my swollen face and bloodshot eyes could be a veritable sign of a divine encounter. Holy snot doesn't sound theologically correct. Maybe though, the holy, if I dare use that word, was how Dad and I held space together in that moment. Or, more accurately put, the way my Dad held me in that space.

Therapy

After my Easter day breakdown, I began seeing a therapist. My wife found him on *Psychology Today*. I liked him instantly. He was a professor by day and therapist by night—like Batman for mental health. It wasn't long before I trusted him enough to drop the act. Most of my life, I felt like I was in the spotlight, performing a role, like a puppet on a string. I don't know if it was a first born thing, or being a PK, or being a youth leader in high school. Maybe it was an amalgamation of all those unspoken pressures. But with my therapist, everything could come out—even the dark dregs. I could say anything, be anything—cynical, angsty, melodramatic, slightly unhinged, even a theological heretic that John Calvin would have burned at the stake.

Never once did my therapist throw holy water on me, try to cast out a demon, or drive a stake through my vampirish heart. We should all be so lucky to have someone like my therapist in our corner.

During one of our sessions, he asked me why I thought I was so depressed and miserable.

"Oh, I don't know. The price of unleaded gas. White-bodied supremacy and my complicity. The loss of KD to the Warriors.

Oklahoma wind. The fungi sprouted on my right long toe. The hitch in my golf swing. My receding hairline. My belly—a hard boiled egg."

I sensed my answers were only scratching the surface. All branches, no roots.

He knew I knew this. I gave him permission to call me on my BS.

"What if the problem is not that you have problems, but that you aren't solving the right problems?"

"Huh? Say more."

He obliged.

"The myth of happiness is that we need to eliminate our problems to be happy. The trick is not to avoid problems or try to eliminate them. No, the challenge is to find the right problems that only you were built to solve."

My therapist added clarity. He wasn't talking about the problems that are just part of life on this floating rock—paying bills, replacing the air conditioner, getting your kid's report card, sharing a cubicle with Toby Flenderson, enduring passive-aggressive jabs from your disapproving mother-in-law, putting down your dog, having a hip replacement.

What he was talking about were the problems that I had signed on the dotted line to solve—the self-chosen ones. My therapist was trying to help me see that there are some problems we aren't built for, no matter how hard we try. And that was okay. You wouldn't want an English teacher in a NASA think tank to fix a spaceship's propulsion system any more than you would want a NASA engineer writing an English curriculum for neurodivergent students. Every day, I was grinding my gears, expending all of my metabolic energy to solve problems that I not only hated solving, but also wasn't naturally hardwired to solve. I felt like I was trying to juggle ten balls with one hand and a pinkie finger. The truth was, there were people out there who were not only good at the stuff I was bad at, but actually loved the shit—natural, two-handed, ten-fingered jugglers. What I was good at was solving problems that involved kids, older teenage kids to be more exact. I loved helping students understand complex ideas in beautifully written books. I loved helping a student find their voice in their writing. I loved cooking up a lesson plan that made Shakespeare not suck. I loved advocating for a kid with a less-than-stellar transcript to a college for admission. I loved helping a student "red-line lower" when their "lizard brain" lid had flipped. Hell, I even loved mediating a compromise between a senior who wanted a gap year in Patagonia and parents who wanted a state university.

What my therapist wanted me to see was that what I did at work was a kind of problem solving. I just didn't see any of it as problem-solving. It's like the parable that David Foster Wallace tells about two fish:

There are these two young fish swimming along and they happen to meet an older fish swimming the other way, who nods at them and says "Morning, boys. How's the water?" And the two young fish swim on for a bit, and then eventually one of them looks over at the other and goes, "What the hell is water?"

My Therapist Helped Me Realize

My therapist helped me realize that what I loved doing was solving problems that weren't even problems to me. My problem, then, was that I was solving the wrong problems. I was a fish out of water.

Post-Apocalyptic Doom

One of the key symptoms of depression is to feel *nothing* but a premonition of doom. The world inside of you feels empty, vacuous, and devoid of hope. Through your blood-red eyes, you see a reality akin to living inside a Cormac McCarthy post-apocalyptic novel, full of ash, soot, and psychopaths.

Growing up in Colorado, I remember passing through the Eisenhower Tunnel on I-70 on our way up to Keystone to ski. I sometimes wondered what would happen if, while we were traveling through the mountainous bowels of Loveland Pass, an avalanche blocked both ends of the tunnel. That's what I felt most days—trapped inside a tunnel. No backend. No frontend. Just darkness. If I could have only known that eventually one end of the tunnel would clear, and a way out would be made possible. Then I could have faced the light.

Depression has a sick pathology. It lies to us. We are gaslighted into thinking something is wrong. But make no mistake—depression itself isn't a lie. It is the most real thing I've ever experienced, like a nightmare. The blistering rub, though, is the fact that depression is an invisible reality, like atoms, particles, and quarks. And that's fucking annoying.

Depression is [Fill in the Blank]

A bedlam.

A brain fog.

A tormenting raven.

Alcatraz prison.

Arrakis.

A black silence.

A doomed vessel, sinking.

Franny's character in Salinger's novel *Franny and Zooey*.

An absence in presence, a menacing paradox.

A sadistic looping algorithm.

The ashy detritus world between

East and West Egg and NYC.

An existential vacuum.

A crystal ball of future

immutability.

Carbonite.

Winterfell.

Waking up a bug.

A violent weather system—tornadoes, hurricanes, dust storms, torrential rain.

The Nothing.

The feeling of drowning.
A brain on fire.

The color of dishwater.
A gas chamber.

A pressure cooker.
A black dog.
Bill Murray's character
in *Rushmore*.
Bill Murray's character in *Lost in Translation*.
Scarlett Johansson's character in *Lost in Translation*.
A civil war between ancient mythology and modern evolutionary biology.

Thin, slippery, cracking ice. A lonely, strange, bony, judgmental girl at the attic window. Gettysburg, a never end battle.
A long dark never ending tunnel.
A thing without feathers.

A painful, invisible infirmity.

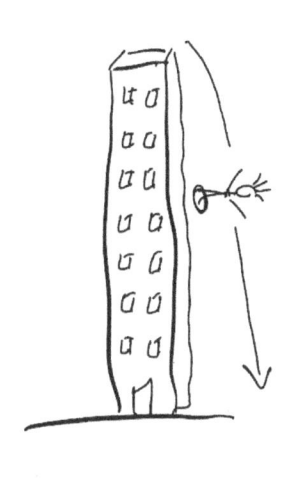

A living nightmare.
Falling.

Armeggedon in the amygdala.
Steam on a bathroom mirror that your face disappears into.
Hikikomori.
Picasso's Blue Period.
A black wormhole of infinitude.
A mortality head clock—tick tock.

Slowly drifting out into the deep sea while people wave on the shoreline.
A dragon.

A dark wood of mottled trees.
A black box.
Mordor.
Mud.
A Chicago winter.

Carcasses Coal Mine, Pit #7.

Sleeping in a cage with a tiger.

A ballad by Amy Winehouse.

A shadowland.

A silent scream.

A waking coma.
A bell jar.
A cuckoo's nest.
Uranus.
A remote jungle island of apeshit crazy guerillas.

"A tale told by an idiot."
Absurdist comedy, Don Delillo-style.

A terminal point of deterministic inevitability.

Dark matter.

The Upside Down world.

Yellow wallpaper.

An abyss.

A cave of gloom.

A corn maze, blindfolded.

A psychosomatic shit show.

Dark Light or Light Dark?

Philosophers, theologians, artists, writers and pretty much anyone who has drawn breath have been asking the same through-line question.

Which is it?

A world and reality of darkness with occasional pin pricks of subatomic light.

?

Or a world and reality with pin pricks of subatomic darkness surrounded by a deeper reality of swirling light?

It feels like believing in the latter requires you to participate in an ayahuasca ritual, or take shrooms with Aaron Rogers on a darkness retreat, or make a pilgrimage to Houston to see Joel Olsteen live, or trek out to the desert to see U2 at The Sphere.

Depression can only imagine a world of darkness. The only small whorls of light are those moments where we pass through a portal that plunges us into a world of artificial lighting—social media, shopping, porn, food, drugs, sleep, vodka tonics, *Friends* reruns, DraftKings sports bets, Expedia scrolls for our next Caribbean vacation.

In the Genesis creation myth, the story goes that in the beginning there was *tohu va-vohu*. The Hebrew translation is wild and waste—a kind of void and nothingness. Most days we wake up with *tohuvavohu* lodged in our intestines. We are stomach-sick from our doomsday scrolling binges, conspiracy theories, 24-hour news cycles, zombie shows, Pulitzers, and vampire porn. There seems little need to explain. If darkness is meant to suggest a world where nobody can see well—either themselves, or each other, or what direction they are heading in, or even where they are standing at the moment; if darkness is meant to convey a sense of uncertainty, of feeling lost, of being terrified, of experiencing a kind of epistemic vertigo; if darkness suggests polarization and division, between races, political parties, nations, and individuals each pretty much out for their own skin—then we live in a world where our imaginations and cities, schools, and homes have been filled with darkness.

If we are people who hold prayer beads or utter words to God in this God-forsaken world, darkness is apt to be a lot of what we mutter under our breath. If we are people who flushed our prayer beads down the toilet, it is likely darkness in one menacing form or another that was responsible.

Some Facts

When you feel like Fortunato in a dark and dank wine cellar, chained up and trapped behind a wall of something that feels so unreal, you look for anything that can give you a shred of sanity and sense of orientation. You crave knowledge. You hunger for facts. You become a data nerd who suddenly likes spreadsheets, bullet points, and pie charts. The data becomes a life vest in a tempest. But statistics, like anything else, can be tricky in the hands of humans.

Things that occur in the mind can often remain hidden under the surface, like icebergs. When I first became mentally ill, I spent a lot of energy feigning normalcy. That's the name of the game, especially when you spend most of your workday in an environment where parents fork over big bucks to have you educate their child. They don't want a head case preparing their kid for college. It's okay to teach about Holden Caulfield's mental illness, but it is not okay to be Holden Caulfield. People often struggle to know how to invite others into their struggles with depression, especially if you are a guy. Also, over time, facts change. Depression didn't used to be depression. It used to be melancholia, and far fewer people suffered from that than they do from current depression. But did they really? Or are people more open and honest about such things now?

Some Facts about Suicide:

- Suicide is the eleventh leading cause of death in the United States. You may think that isn't horrible. Well, consider that suicide was the second leading cause of death among individuals between the ages of 10-14 and 25-34 , the third leading cause of death among individuals between the ages of 15-24, and the fifth leading cause of death among individuals between the ages of 35 and 44.

- Suicide is the leading cause of death among men under the age of thirty-five.

- There were nearly two times as many suicides in the United States as there were homicides.

- Suicidal thoughts are highest among young adults ages 18-28.

- In 2022, suicide rates vary widely depending on where you are in the world. For example, in my state, Oklahoma, there are 20.61+ suicides per 100,000 deaths, as opposed to New York where there are 0-13.18 suicides per 100,000 deaths. If you live in the mountain kingdom of Lesotho in South

Africa, you are thirty more times more likely to kill yourself than if you lived in Artigua and Barbuda.

- In 2022, 13.2 million adults had serious thoughts of suicide, 3.8 million adults made suicide plans, and 1.6 million adults attempted suicide.

Some Facts about Depression:

- One in five people gets depression at some point in their life. More than that will suffer from mental illness.

- Antidepressants are on the rise. Monthly antidepressant prescriptions jumped 66% between 2016 and 2022. After the pandemic spread, from March 2020, prescriptions rose more than 63%.

- Antidepressants rose 64% among teenagers during the pandemic.

- Twice as many women as men will suffer a serious bout of depression in their lives.

- Combined depression and anxiety are the most common in the US and UK, followed by anxiety, posttraumatic stress disorder, "pure" depression, phobias, eating disorders, OCD, and panic disorder.

- Women are more likely to seek and receive treatment for mental health problems than men.

- The risk of developing depression is about 40% if a biological parent has been diagnosed with the illness.

Toxicified Men

Out of curiosity, I did a simple Google engine search and typed in "toxic masculinity." I got a mere 17,600,000 hits. Consequently, back in 2018, *toxic* was named the Oxford Dictionary Word of the Year. I imagine *toxic* could win that award pretty much every year now, like Brad Pitt and *People's* Sexiest Man of the Year award. In my narrow and limited perspective, it seems that toxic masculinity in our culture today flows both ways, like the Hudson Estuary—out of men, for sure, but also into men. It's the chicken-and-egg problem. Toxic and toxicified masculinity are incestuously interrelated, kin of the same rotting flesh and bone and progeny. At the heart of the problem is a social construct that is soulsick.

The data is well documented to support this claim.

- A staggeringly higher number of men than women kill themselves. The suicide rate among males was approximately four times higher than the rate among females.

- Males make up 50% of the population but nearly 80% of suicides.

- In the UK, the ratio is 3:1; in Greece 3:1; in the USA, 4:1. According to the World Health Organization, the only countries in the world where more women kill themselves than men kill themselves are China and Hong Kong. Everywhere else, many more men than women end their own lives. This is especially strange when researchers have known for years that women are about twice as likely to be diagnosed with depression as men.

The fact is that in most places in the world, there is something about being a man that makes you more prone to kill yourself. And there is also this head-scratching paradox: If suicide is a symptom of depression, then why do more women suffer depression than men? Why, in other words, is depression more fatal if you are a man rather than a woman?

This then begs the question: Why do so many men kill themselves? What has gone awry?

The common answer is that men, traditionally, see mental illness as a signifier of masculine weakness. As a result, we are more reluctant to seek help. Our natural tendency is to repress emotion instead of express it, and to mimic a kind of stoicism that stretches all the way back to Troy. The dominant message from Greco-

Roman times is the same message we receive today—to be vulnerable is to be weak, and to be weak is to get yourself eaten alive in our pitbull-eat-pitbull world. Not long ago, I watched the Netflix miniseries *A Man in Full*, starring Jeff Daniels as Charlie Crocker—a Southern business tycoon, Trumpian-like, larger-than-life; a man's-man who fights rattlesnakes with his bare hands. In one revealing scene, Crocker has to get a robotic knee, and he says to his wife, "I don't mind turning 60, I mind being weak. I can not be weak." There it is. The one thing men can't be in our society— perceived weak, because in our social Darwinian ethos, we are all environmentally conditioned into a construct like Charlie Crocker to believe that we are biologically hardwired by natural selection and survival-of-the-fittest ethical norms to stave off weakness of any kind. Our survival depends upon it. We must adapt to the kind of masculine construct that will help us survive, though not necessarily thrive.

But let's pressure-test this kind of gender construct with data generated from within the United States.

- Let's begin with gender ratios for school suspensions and expulsions. About 51% of the students in the 72,000 schools that made up the Department of Education's database were female. But 64% of all students who were suspended were males. Some 69% of all students suspended from school more than once were male, as were 74% of all students expelled from school.

- Next, the gender ratio in our current prison system. According to the most recent numbers published by the Federal Bureau of Prisons (BOP), 93.2% of the approximately 185,500 federal inmates are men; only 6.8% are women.

- How about the predominant gender pulling the trigger on mass shootings? Since 1982, an astonishing 143 mass shootings have been carried out in the United States by male shooters. In contrast, only four mass shootings (defined by the source as a single attack in a public place in which four or more victims were killed) have been carried out by women.

We are paying the consequences for a dominant masculine construct that has long neglected men's mental health. We suffer from what Yale theologian William James Jennings calls a *diseased imagination.* It is long overdue for a new masculine overstory, one that makes attending to and caring for one's mental health a normative part of what it means to pursue healthy masculinity.

See-Saws and Dark Matter

Roughly 1 in 10 Americans over age 12 takes antidepressants.

I am one of those 1 out of 10 Americans.

This is what feels double-edged. In one sense, I'm disheartened, if not envious. I'd love it if I were one of the nine who didn't begin their day with an antidepressant cocktail mix of bupropion, desvenlafaxine, and clonazepam. It doesn't help that the names of these drugs sound like an alien species about to attack the USS Enterprise on *Star Trek*. It's not a great feeling knowing that every day I take antidepressants, I'm making a small contribution to the over $678 billion in annual big pharmaceutical sales in the U.S., even if I am just a gluon in that lucrative universe. Not to mention, I feel the jagged edge of my hypocrisy, knowing that every time I take 300 mg of this and 100 mg of that, I'm doing my capitalistic duty for society, swallowing down the whole idea that everything has a quick fix by consuming things. But in another sense, I'm really grateful that I live in a time where we've made huge breakthroughs in brain science and psychiatry. Neurotransmitters and neural pathways, as well as serotonin and dopamine levels, have become a part of the lingua franca of our zeitgeist. Brain research has helped us discover that our brains work a lot like a see-saw. When dopamine levels get out of balance in our brains, and see-saw downward, we see a spike in depressive symptoms like apathy, listlessness, body lethargy, and feelings of hopelessness. If our serotonin levels see-saw down, we see a bio-emotional downswing often resulting in low vibrations, moodiness, sleep disruption, and impaired cognition. Thanks to the meds I take each day, my see-saw brain is able to strike a better balance, which in turn helps me concentrate better, think more clearly, talk more coherently, and move through the day with some semblance of equilibrium, keeping the gremlins at bay.

A friend of mine recently asked me if I plan to stay on meds for the rest of my life. Honestly, I don't know. I am reminded most days that this thing in our heads weighs only a little over a kilogram, and yet it contains a universe—literally. It is, like everything else, made out of atoms and particles, which themselves came into being in stars millions, if not billions, of years ago. Yet, we know more about the stars in our galaxies than we do the processes in our brains, which is ironic because the one thing in the whole universe that can think about the whole universe is, in fact, our brains. All I know is that before I began taking antidepressant medication, I was in a constant state of brain fog, with a low, enervating hum of consciousness. Most days, I felt like I was floating outside of my body, like an astronaut in outer space, drifting farther and farther away into deep space until I could no longer see the Earth's oblate spheroid shape. Now, though, thanks to the meds, I feel much more grounded and energized, lucid and clear-headed, a citizen of planet Earth again, no longer a Klingon on Qo'nos.

The more you research the brain science of depression, the more you realize that it is still characterized by what we don't know than what we do know, like dark matter. It is 90% mystery and unknowing, which is a fucking pain. One thing for sure, though, is that we are nowhere near the far edges of neuroscience—it is maybe one of the last frontiers. Which means that it is only a matter of time before what we know now about the brain is debunked and labeled under the same bogus category as flat earth theory and the geocentric models of the Earth. That is how science works—not through blind faith, but through sound reason, scientific methodology, and continued spirals of skepticism.

To that end, when it comes to what we do in the here-and-now, I'm not entirely sure I've got the full answer. The best I've come up with is to try and block out the white noise and listen to my own life. For me, I'm a meds guy, shamelessly and pragmatically. Up to this point, meds have worked, and frankly, I don't need to know why something works, just if it works. That might be sloppy consumerism, but, honestly, I just don't give a shit. My position now is much more heterodox. If it works, do it. If it keeps you sane, do it. If it keeps you alive, do it. If it gives you even a modicum of hope, do it. Whether it's hypnosis or yoga or CDC gummies or transcendental meditation or cognitive behavioral therapy or homeopathy or EMDR or antidepressant medication or micro-dosing mushrooms or some combination of any or all of these things.

For me, I do what I know keeps the see-saw levels balanced, so that I can stay married, employed, out of jail, and free from the white coats at the Hawkins National Laboratory. I hope you do the same, because at some point, we have to trust in our own personal laboratory of trial and error, especially in the absence of any kind of universal certainty and conclusiveness on this strange and mysterious planet.

Green, Yellow, Red

Months of therapy culminated in one shimmering didactic moment with my dad. In his earthly wisdom, dad explained to me his three colors analogy in regard to work.

First, there's green. The color of flourishing. The feeling of yawp, Mr. Keatings in his classroom or Mr. Holland in the band room—the sweet spot. As my dad would say, green is work we love to do that does a lot of good.

Second, there's yellow. The color of survival. The feeling of meh, some hybrid between Homer Simpson and Andrea Sachs. We do the work with a low, mundane hum of anxiety, ennui, and malaise.

And third, there's red. The color
of crisis. The feeling of fuck.
That's Peter Gibbons at Initech
with Bill Lumberg hovering
over your cubicle, waiting for
the newest TPS report while
sipping on coffee in his "I'm Boss" mug.

Dad had diagnosed my conundrum. My days had become 5% green, 10% yellow, and 85% red—Quinten Tarantino red. I had watched every verdant blade of vitality mower-clipped, raked up, and black bagged—hobbits in Middle-earth,

giggly teenage laughter in the school hallways, and the *eurekajoy* moments when an idea clicked for a student.

Dad had helped me see that I was on a perilous trajectory. I had to take action—the kind that involved meeting with my boss and telling my boss that I was in the danger zone.

The Meeting

I lay awake all night working out my spiel. With a choreographed plan, I would walk into my boss's office dressed in my best J. Crew Ludlow power suit and get down to business.

I got about a sentence in before I lost it. Like looooooosssssssssttttttt my shhhhhhiiiiiiittttttt!

I sobbed and snotted all over my Ludlow suit sleeve, head buried in my arm, concealing my ugly cry face.

A minute or so passed.

I felt a gentle nudge with a tissue. I took it and blew my nose. Eventually, I straightened up, rubbed my puffy eyes, and took a deep breath. I feared that when I looked up my boss would be staring at me as though I was some extraterrestrial from Area 51.

One of the superpowers of my boss was his ability to be fully present. In that vulnerable moment, he switched into a kind of *eternal-now* state of consciousness. His eyes were gentle, rimmed with compassion. For the next hour, he let me "red"-catharsis-vomit, never once interrupting me. He just sat and listened with quiet attention. His heart in his ears.

My boss and I had many more conversations in the aftermath of my melt down. That was a watershed moment for us. A shift truly occurred between us. My boss went from Iceman the rival to Iceman the wingman. Through every heart-to-heart conversation, my boss helped pull me out of my redspiral, and, over time, plopped me down in a greenspace.

That lush green space-time at work lasted about as long as it took you to read these words.

The Call You're Never Prepared For

We've all had moments in the flow of chronos time when we know exactly where we were when something unexpected came roaring around the bend, the undercurrent hurling us downstream, all the while, gashing us against the jaggedrockbed, leaving permanent scars on the skin of our memory.

January 28, 1986. I was 8. The Spaceship Challenger and the seven astronauts inside the rocket disappeared inside a glowing ball of fire and smoke.

November 7, 1991. I was 16. Magic Johnson, my boyhood hero, announced his retirement effective immediately. He had been diagnosed with HIV.

April 19, 1995. I was 19. In my dorm room, I watched firemen and police officers and emergency medics scramble in horror, looking for survivors in the smoking rubble of the Murrah Federal Building in Oklahoma City, my childhood home.

These kinds of chronos moments certainly mark the course of our lives, though they don't necessarily alter the course of our lives. We feel the gravitas of them, from a distance, indirectly. But the moments that alter our lives are the ones where we are at ground zero, the epicenter, directly in the path of the cyclone.

February 18, 2020. I was 44. As I headed to lunch, I got a call from my boss. He was in Philadelphia at a national conference. He didn't have long to talk. He told me Covid-19 was coming. There'd been a confirmed case in the States. My mind started to glitch. I caught fragments of his words—pandemic...wildfire...total shutdown.

"Josh, we've got four weeks to prepare."

"Prepare to do what?"

"I don't have time to talk at length, Josh."

"Okay, what do you want me to do?"

"I want you to get the directors together and start building a plan."

"Again, a plan for what?"

"A virtual school, Josh."

"Did you say a virtual school?"

"That's right. After spring break, we will most likely go online."

"Okay."

"Thanks, Josh. Talk to you soon."

I sat down on a bench, my chest tightening. I closed my eyes, concentrating on my breath. Just breathe.

I was in a bad dream and would wake up soon.

Things I Never Thought I'd Say as a Teacher|Administrator

(But Did Say Thanks to COVID)

Please keep your camera on during class at all times.

I understand you don't know how to teach your child $a^2 - b^2 = (a-b)(a+b)$.

Is that the Millenium Falcon? (Zoom backdrop)

It's okay if you hold your one-year-old while you teach Spanish.

Please come to class with a shirt on.

The chat box is for analysis, not SpongeBob memes.

Hey, excuse me, you aren't muted. I can hear you telling your parents that you aren't learning anything in my class.

Please don't take your laptop into the bathroom during class.

I understand that you can't teach Spanish with the mask on.

I am sorry that you think that requiring your child to wear a mask borders on child abuse.

Is that your dog barking? What kind of dog is it?

Is that Andy's bedroom from *Toy Story?* (Zoom backdrop)

I know you didn't sign up to teach in a virtual school. I didn't sign up to run a virtual school.

The Covid Antidepressant

Covid-19 plunged much of the world into a mental health crisis. The World Health Organization reported a 25% increase in prevalence of anxiety and depression worldwide. That's 1 out of 4 people. Alarming statistic, for sure. And yet, not surprising. We are social animals, after all. As Brene Brown puts it, we are hardwired for connection. Isolation, fear, and the horror show that was the 24-hour news cycle of body counts and new case reports—it's no wonder then that there was a major spike in mental unhealth.

I was no different. The struggle was real.

Noö-Dynamics

I used to teach a senior seminar titled *Quest and Questions.* It was an interdisciplinary course that integrated multiple disciplines, ranging from literature and history to psychology and philosophy. One of the books we read in this seminar was Victor Frankl's Holocaust memoir *Man's Search for Meaning*. Frankl argues in the book that the primary human drive is not pleasure (Freud), power (Nietzsche), or wealth (Marx), but the pursuit of meaning (*logos*).

Frankl writes:
What man actually needs is not a tensionless state but rather the striving and struggling for a worthwhile goal, a freely chosen task. What he needs is not the discharge of tension at any cost but the call of a potential meaning waiting to be fulfilled by him. What man needs is not homeostasis but what I call noö-dynamics, i.e., the existential dynamics in a polar field of tension where one pole is represented by a meaning that is to be fulfilled and the other pole by the man who has to fulfill it.

Often, I'd read this passage twice to my students. It was doozy...and hence, a call for doodling!

After I put the black marker down, I explained to my students: According to Frankl, if our goal is to homeostasis-ize our lives by creating poles of existence that include a smooth path forward that eliminates all stress, pain, and struggle, we will actually regress, de-evolve, and downslide in fulfilling our human potential.

That's when I'd redraw the doodle of the slant and then add to it.

Just like with quest stories, Frankl argues that what our lives need is a metanarrative of valiant struggle shaped by *logos* and *telos*. Without meaning (*logos*) and purpose (*telos*), our lives fail to experience self-actualization and self-transcendence.

I then juxtaposed the slant line doodle with a flat line doodle.

I explained to my students that our natural impulse is to gravitate toward the flat story, even though our hearts ache for the slant story. Imagine what a story would be like without struggle, challenge, conflict. Imagine *The Avengers* without Thanos. Or the *Mario Brothers* video games without Bowser. Or *Game of Thrones* without that bad-ass scene where Arya Stark comes hurling through the air and plunges her steel blade through the fucking iceheart of the Night King.

At this point in the lecture, I would often pull up a chair in front of my students, sit down in it and look them all in the eyes. In that moment, I'd tell them how the flat line story has mostly dominated my own life story. Truth is, I've always been risk allergic. Anti-noö-dynamics-y. I want to blame the birthing order. I am a first born after all, genetically hardwired for caution and reticence. I was the kid, for example, in dodgeball games who hung back on the baseline and let the other schmucks get blasted first. Growing up in Oklahoma, if you had a sliver of athleticism, you were expected to play football—from peewee leagues to Friday night lights. I was a holdout due to my scrawny frame, thank God. I blamed my parents, but secretly, I thanked them. I strapped on the pads for the first time in 7th grade. After the first practice, I realized something important about football: I didn't like tackling. At all.

I wish I could tell my students that I grew out of the flat line mentality the way I grew out of my size nine basketball shoes in

7th grade. I wish I could tell them that with adulthood comes a new noö-dynamic growth spurt.

Carl Jung talks about the shadow self, this negative energy that flows like lava in the subterranean regions of our consciousness. The shadow self almost always operates out of a consciousness of fear.

At some point, Jung argues we must confront the shadow. I wrap up my lecture by telling my students, "I don't know about you, but I'd rather just rent *The Empire Strikes Back* and watch Luke confront his shadow in Darth Vader instead."

The Multiphrenic Self

If I'm honest with you (not my students), my shadow self is a multiphrenic self. The prefix *multi* means many, variegated, more than one. It's my many-ness that shames me. It's seeing myself in the dark as the incompetent self. The incapable self. The impotent self with low sperm. The self that can't fix a light fixture. The self that gets thrown over the handlebars of a moped scooter, face-planting right in front of his wife, son, and in-laws. The self that failed 6th grade-phonics and mispronounces words like Michael Scott does. The self that can't do what people expect me to do, especially the people I admire and respect: my wife, my son, my parents, my siblings, my boss.

I remember telling my therapist that I was tired of pretending. The whole "fake it until you make it" thing was just too damn exhausting. All I wanted to do was come out from behind myself and show people my real self. My therapist looked at me and said, "Well, what's stopping you from doing that?" The truth was, me. I was stopping myself. I didn't want to risk what waited for me on the other side of the vulnerability. It harkens back to Victor Frankl and his concept of *noö-dynamics*. I wanted a pathway to a pole without a slant. I wanted to remain a dodgy fucker, the kind of person who avoids the kind of risk that puts me directly in the line of fire from people around me. I didn't want to face my inner Darth Vader.

A Nebulous Omen

December 2017. I'm not a superstitious person. Or into astrology like my wife. When it's Mercury Retrograde, especially in July because my water-sign is Cancer, my wife will caution me to avoid any big decisions, like quitting my job to pursue stand-up comedy or getting a puppy. I've learned from her that when we're in Mercury Retrograde, the planets take a snooze, and during that hibernate astrological time, we're kind of on our own, unsupervised, and, therefore, vulnerable to pandemonium.

Our house has these big panel windows in the living room that look out onto a backyard green belt where trees sprawl and birds perch. On occasion, a bird will *beak-crash* into the back porch window. They see our Majesty Palm reflected in the window and mistake it for the simulacrum.

Six a.m., the season of the winter solstice. Fumbling in the early morning semi-darkness, I turned on a living room light. My family was still asleep. My thoughts raced, even without coffee lubricating my brain. Today, I had a huge presentation to the Board of Trustees on a new initiative—one I'd been working on with a team for about a year in my new role as Associate Head of Academics.

Flashback a year: While exiting a Trustees meeting after a different presentation, the Board Chair bellowed under his thick beard, "Josh, innovate. That's your charge from us." I had been the Associate Head for less than a month. At the moment, it was clear that I was hired to lead change, to be a change agent. My primary responsibility was to oversee, lead, and manage major institutional disruption. The Chair's one-worded charge served as another inciting incident for me, a disorienting jettisoning into the scary but necessary unknown.

And here's why.

The school was seventy-four years old and synonymous with Tradition with a capital *T*. The school's founders envisioned a New England-style prep school built up around the oil rigs outside of Oklahoma City. In my mind, the Trustees were asking me to create a Dalmatian-like T with spots of Innovation. My presentation on that frosty December morning involved casting a vision for the first spot of our strategic academic plan: a new Interdisciplinary Studies Program.

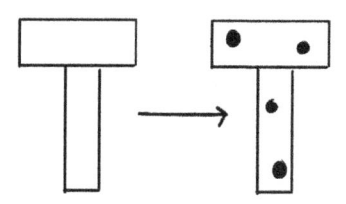

Back to the living room, during the first yawn of sunlight. While putting on my socks and shoes, I heard a thud on our backyard window. Not a bird-thud though. A *splat-thud*, like a watermelon. I turned on the back porch lights and discovered an owl, swaying woozy-like. It looked concussed, like it just absorbed a haymaker from Mike Tyson. The dog broke feral. My wife and son rushed into the living room, joining me in sleepy-eyed disbelief at the owl perched on the back porch sofa.

The owl and I locked eyes.

The obsidian discs of the creature had a menace to them, a gothicness, a macabre quality.

"I'm pretty sure this is a bad omen for my presentation today, family."

"Or a good one, Dad."

Come to find out, my son had a point. In Japanese culture, the owl symbolizes inner wisdom, change, transformation, intuitive development, and good luck. However, also come to find out, in other cultures owls symbolize bad juju. Take the Apache tribe: owls are bearers of bad omens, harbingers of impending doom, or even symbols of death itself.

Eventually, the owl flew away, and my son and I headed off to school. All day before the presentation, the owl's haunting silhouette remained perched in the back of my skull, staring at me with the blackmidnight eyes of Poe's ominous raven.

"Nevermore."

"Nevermore."

"Never…"

"Oh, shut the fuck up, bird."

Anxiety is [Fill in the Blank]

An asteroid breaking through the earth's atmosphere.

Dark clouds over shark infested waters.

A child with colic on an airplane.

Breathing through a coffee stirrer.

Biting off your fingernails.

MRI machines.

The loss of control.

The Doomsday Clock.

Screaming under water.

Fox News.

CNN.

Most clowns.

A banana tree full of jumping monkeys.

The world of Margaret Atwood's *The Handmaid's Tale*.

Airport security.

Flying American Airlines into DFW.

Taking communion at an Episcopal Church.

Smoke detectors going off in the middle of the night.

Bad meat-lovers pizza.

24,541—the number of my wife's unread emails.

Two roads diverged into a yellow wood.

The new mole on my back.

A nightmare where you're being chased by

Freddy Krueger and your mother-in-law.

Watching a presidential debate.

My 403b retirement portfolio.

Motorcyclists on highways without helmets.

Tornado sirens wailing through the night.

Back spasms before public speaking.

Deadlines.

Finding clothes that fit.

Flying over the ocean.

A phone call after 8 p.m. from your boss.

Rapture theology.

Needles.

The snake house at the zoo.

Mammograms.

Turning 50 and my upcoming proctology exam with Dr. Jellyfingers.

Progress Notes from teachers.

The rising cost of college tuition.

My 75-year old dad with his titanium hip replacement—playing pickleball.

Stuck in an elevator with Bob Wiley.

Anything by Kurt Vonnegut.

Getting ghosted by a friend.

Scantron tests.

SAT test results.

Ivy League admissions rates.

The cross and flag.

The ER in downtown Oklahoma City.

A cancer diagnosis.

The theme music of *Jaws*.

The ocean.

Velociraptors in *Jurassic Park*.

Judgment Day—Sheep or goat?

Waiting for the other shoe to drop.

Your annual job review.

A canker sore.

April 15th.

An involuntary face paroxysm.

The unknown.

Episode 6 of Season 2 in *The Bear*—Carmy's Christmas Eve dinner with the family.

Pretty much the whole Old Testament minus a few Psalms and the Song of Solomon.

World War II movies.

An empty nest.

Las Vegas casinos.

Your husband is posting selfies.

Black Friday at Wal-Mart.

The Mall of America.

Sauna rooms.

Amusement rides that spin whirl corkscrew loop.

Losing your wallet—driver's license, insurance card, credit cards, the free Andy's custard coupon.

Asking Siri for directions to the Hollywood sign in LA.

The evolving scale of AI.

A future without my family.

The Hero's Journey—The Call to Adventure

Psychologist Joseph Campbell famously gave us the archetype of the hero's journey. The journey begins with the call to adventure. It's the stage of the journey where the hero must say goodbye to the status quo and cloistered familiarity, leaving the known world for the unknown world.

The owl's visit months earlier was a good omen. A Japanese owl, after all.

The Board presentation went well. I even got applause from the suits—a rarity.

Now it was time to take our plans public, starting with our faculty and staff.

Gulp.

You have to understand: most teachers are allergic to change, like peanut-allergy allergic. We prickle like porcupines at the adminspeak of things like new initiatives. Put truth serum in them, and most teachers see administrators as a nuisance, like a hungry fly near their egg salad sandwich. I can understand and empathize. We work really hard to map out our curriculum, design our lesson plans, master our content, and create a system and mechanism and set of levers that streamlines everything in an efficient way. The last thing we want is an ambitious, ladder-climbing carpetbagger administrator to come in and fuck everything up. This is why, when it comes to the innovation curve, teachers tend to land on the right side of that curve. We adopt and adapt to innovation at a very slow pace—like a family of manatees. Then there's me. I've always been more of a peregrine falcon—a creature of constant flight, movement, speed, evolution, change. I'm perpetually seeking the bleeding edge of innovation. Which, for an administrator, can also be a headache. Some change is okay. A lot of change is not because it throws the whole ecosystem into a state of disequilibrium. So herein was the challenge for me: to lead the school into a space and place of innovation, as charged by the Board Chair and Trustees, at a pace and clip that moved my whole beautiful manatee family forward at a speed that didn't harm their morale or crash their systems of competency.

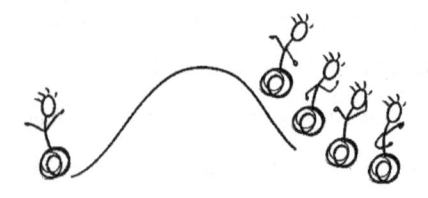

This would be a Cha-Cha dance, for sure.

Standing center stage in the Fee Theater, I would deliver my inaugural speech on the Interdisciplinary Studies Program, as well as our larger, overarching Strategic Academic Plan (SAP). This was a threshold moment—a crossing over the Rubicon from Josh as *colleague* to Josh as *administrator*. My boss had tasked me with orienting and inspiring the faculty around the SAP. I could do this. I had to do this. This was why I had been hired: for moments like these. I'd spoken at pep rallies, delivered pre-game talks in the locker room, and gotten many kids over the years to stand on their desks and yawp.

But this was something different.

In my opening slide, I clicked on an image of Joseph Campbell's monomyth of the hero's journey and went into full warpaint William Wallace mode of elocution. I told my colleagues that we'd been summoned to a mission. A serious choice stood before us. We could remain in our hobbit holes and cleave to the status quo. Or we could gather our collective courage and blaze out like all of the great heroes of the stories we love—Frodo and Sam, Katniss Everdeen, Luke Skywalker, Harry Potter, Rey, Paul Atreides, Anna—crossing the Rubicon into the unknown.

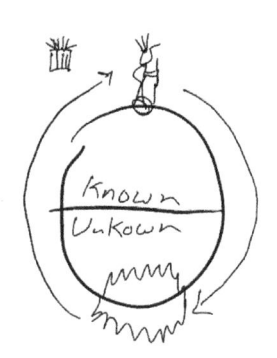

From there, I transitioned to the strategic work ahead of us: new daily schedule, new curriculum, cutting edge pedagogy. Yes, we would be pushed out of our comfort zone. And yes—there may even be times we will want to quit and go work at Starbucks or get a job as a ski instructor in Vail. But nothing great had ever been accomplished without valiant struggle. And what we were summoned to was something great because it was about our kids and their futures.

Lastly, I talked about what psychologist William Hodges calls the "zone of disequilibrium." Anytime an institution goes on a journey that involves a process of significant change and disruption, we will inevitably pass through a liminal space of uncertainty. In that place, our natural human impulse will want a clean, straight line through to safety—a pathway of no tension, no variance, no strain or discomfort. But as Hodges points out, often the pathway of real growth—for institutions and for individuals—involves a messy, squiggly line. And no matter whether you are leading the change through that zone of disequilibrium or following the leader through the disruption—it sucks for everyone.

So, my colleagues and friends, who is coming with me? I actually said that. My Oscar scene. My Jerry Maguire moment, hands out, goldfish in hand, waving them toward me. As I dropped the mic and exited stage left, I swear I heard a thunder roar of applause. It could also have been an artificial sound I heard in the echo chamber of my head.

The Hero's Journey—The Descent

The faculty presentation had laid the groundwork for the hero's journey ahead of us. Greenlit by the Trustees, a small band of us embarked on a quest into the unknown to create a new, beyond-the-AP, 11th-grade interdisciplinary, team-taught, design-thinking-based course called *American Design*.

We unveiled the Interdisciplinary Studies Program to our community in a town hall meeting. The initial feedback from parents, faculty, and students was about 90-ish% positive.

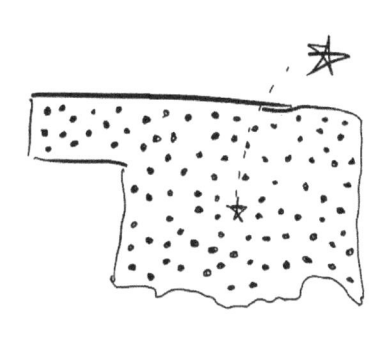

We had successfully announced our voyage. We were embarked, setting sail to take our English and history programs beyond the AP curriculum into unchartered, adventurous waters. Three hundred thirty-eight schools in Oklahoma offered AP curriculum. We would be one of the first schools in Oklahoma to offer something beyond AP, moving our humanities program toward a new North Star.

In my mind, after the town hall, it would be smooth sailing.

I was so fucking Buddy-the-Elf naive.

I had forgotten that no hero's journey is complete without conflict. Trials inevitably abound, and at some point, the protagonist must face the ultimate test—the abyss. Often, the hero doesn't see it coming. It's the scene early on in *Fellowship of the Rings,* where, under the camouflage of night, the Ringwraiths advance on Frodo and his fellow hobbits at Weathertop.

What ambushed me and my team came from a wraith world—a triad of Nazgul that none of us could have fortified ourselves against.

COVID.

Critical race theory.

The Capitol riot.

Before we knew it, the Interdisciplinary Studies Program had gotten sucked up into the unctuous vortex of the zeitgeist. We were in a rapid state of descent inside our school's gates.

What we feared most in that downward movement was that we were losing the community's trust and faith in us and our futuristic vision.

The conspiracy theories swept through our community like an Oklahoma prairie fire. In response, some parents demanded cameras in classrooms. Other parents wanted a book audit of the entire Pre-K-12 English curriculum. There was even word of a government-employed parent playing Big Brother, sluicing into each teacher's political party affiliation and voting record. With each day and week, the rhetoric in the community grew more inflammatory. It all felt like a dystopian dream—a terrifying Orwellian nightmare. The accusations alone had polluted the air over the campus, leaving a haze of noxious smog.

American Design is a woke class.

The humanities departments are all a bunch of Marxists.

This Interdisciplinary program is a Trojan Horse for a CRT agenda.

American Design is code for anti-American.

They want our kids to hate America.

By this time, I was reeling. I had been at this school for almost seventeen years. This was my home away from home, my family, the people I loved and cared for deeply. One of the things I loved most about the school's ethos was that we were a big tent community, a safe environment for students and families of all religious, political, ethnic, and sexuality types and stripes. Even as a religious school, we didn't have a formal piety, which allowed us to foster a more pluralistic and inclusive ethos. We were like Spot, the polka-dotted leopard in Dr. Seuss's book *Put Me In the Zoo*. The more dots, the better. At least, I thought that was the case.

For the first time, I felt something new bubbling up through the cracks of the soil—something jetty colored, insidious. I felt unsafe. Even terrified at times. It was though I had landed in the Upside Down, alternate reality in *Stranger Things*, tripping over alien vines, banging my head on floating rocks, and hearing the sound of something predatory stalking me.

The Abyss

The abyss is where all the lights go out. Everything you know disappears. The floor drops out underneath you, and you can feel yourself in a state of freefall, but you can't see the bottom beneath you. You lose all illusions of control. You become powerless against the forces of gravity. The speed and wind rip the clothes right off your body. Helpless, you close your eyes and pray that you don't feel the moment of impact. All is darkness, nakedness, weightlessness, and waiting.

Things Depression Says To You In The Abyss

Welcome to Shawshank.

You might want to put a shirt on. What about *that* are you proud of?

People who poke grizzly bears get eaten by grizzly bears.

With severance or no severance?

Ziprecruiter or Indeed?

I bet your wife is divorce lawyer shopping right now. Better call your brother and lawyer up, big boy.

I'm not even sure the dog would pick you in the settlement.

You once lived in an apartment with only a mattress and a poster of Kramer. You can do it again.

You can always move back in with your parents.
Maybe you can get a job teaching English in Vietnam.

You used to drive a school bus in college. Your CDL license is probably still good.

It's 10:30 p.m. Time for an ice cream sandwich.

Fuck the Peloton.

20 pills should do the trick.

It's not OK to be not OK.

You don't deserve a penis.

The Exact Moment I Entered My Abyss

My boss called and asked me to come see him immediately. The inflection in his voice was tense, coiled tight like steel wire. Before I could sit down in the chair across from his desk, he turned his computer screen toward me. He had my Twitter account pulled up. He pointed to the screen and, like a prosecuting attorney, asked me, "Did you post these tweets?" I could tell from the fidgetiness of his face something was clearly wrong. He pointed again to his computer screen. They were definitely from my Twitter account. Strangely though, they were from back in July. It was now April, nine months later. It took me a moment to recall the context.

It was in the wake of George Floyd's lynching. American streets roiled with protest and outrage. My fourteen-year-old Black son, like so many other African American adolescents, was in the accelerated throes of racialized puberization. My wife and I felt the fear, confusion, and sadness behind his eyes. In that tense moment, Amy and I recalled the basic principle of Trust-Based Relational Parenting (TBRI) from our adoption education. It's all about connection. That's how we care for and help each other heal.

Which brings me to my two reposted tweets.

I found this blog post titled "Black, on the Fourth of July." The author, early on, lets the readers know that he draws inspiration from Frederick Douglas's speech "What to the Slave Is the Fourth of July?" I shared a couple excerpts from Douglas's famous speech with my son. I reminded him that Douglas gave his speech on July 5, 1852 to an audience of mostly white women at the Ladies Anti-Slavery Society of Rochester.

After reading and discussing the blog post with my son, I tweeted two quotes from the post.

Tweet 1:
"I cannot, with any integrity, celebrate the America that existed in 1776. That America was one steeped in every ist and ism imaginable; laying the foundation for a society by which I am dehumanized on a daily basis. Whether in the overtly institutionalized racism and sexism, or the only somewhat more subtle forms of classism—that America was barely a fully fertilized embryo, an infant of an idea, and yet bigotry was already being warmed as formula in a baby's bottle."

Tweet 2:

"Every current institution of oppression has that America to thank for its existence. Who do we thank for redlining and housing discrimination? Thank the Stars & Stripes. Want to know who's responsible for cultural monetization and appropriation? Good 'ole America the beautiful. Every time a Black or Brown body is beaten, raped, and then vilified without regard for their existence? You guessed it, our founding fathers laid that framework as well. The system is not broken; it's working exactly how it was intended."

I explained the context of the tweets to my boss. He tried to understand and express sympathy, even while his fingers twitched and spasmed. When he got real anxious, he played with his wedding ring. His gold band had not stopped hurling around his right index finger, a hula hoop of agitated motion. He asked me to send him the full article. I did and received a short email of thanks in response. I thought the matter was over.

Little do I know, a hurricane storm coiled like a nautilus whorl out over the deep waters.

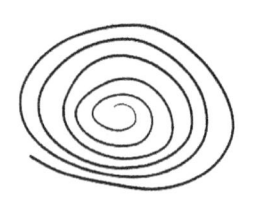

My Kryptonite

I am a people pleaser. Have been for as long as I can remember. It's my kryptonite.

As a kid, I owned a Stretch Armstrong action figurine. I would twist, pull, and stretch the silly puddy doll into all sorts of configurations. As an adult, I felt like Stretch Armstrong most days—twisting, pulling, stretching myself into any figurine that would solicit people's approval, especially those I respected and admired.

As I was growing up, like a lot of kids, my dad was my Superman. I wasn't a good student like he was, so I aspired to be a great athlete like he was. Dad coached me in soccer, baseball, and basketball. The "atta boy" and ritualistic tousle of my strawberry red hair came with netting a goal, dinging a homer, or making a moon ball. These were all ways I could weigh Dad's approval on an invisible scale. By middle school, my compulsion for approval shifted to peers. In the throes of awkward pubescence, I was like Flick in *The Christmas Story*, who once drank a half-bottle of mustard as a triple-dog dare. In high school, I was part-Zach

Morris and part-Waylon Smithers—schmoozer and suck-up—with peers, with teachers, with coaches, with administrators, with youth leaders, with parents.

I wish I could tell you I grew out of all of this in adulthood. I'd be lying. It had been more of the same. My neurosis and addictive impulses were just more subtle and hidden. I counted my likes on social media. I obsessed over my student's course evaluations. I fretted over parent comments in school-wide surveys. I snorted my boss's affirmation like cocaine.

I was an approval junkie. At the end of the day, I was strung out. The whole fetid enterprise, day in and day out, would take its toll. I'd spend many nights in a memory loop in my head, replaying over and over again the moments in my day where I fucked up or failed to bring my A-game.

Schopenhauer once said, *We forfeit three-fourths of ourselves in order to be like other people.*

I felt like I had forfeited nine-tenths of myself to fit into the cardboard box that made everyone around me feel like I was a nice, safe, and likable person—like Mark Ruffalo.

When news began to trickle in of a growing groundswell of protest toward me, I went into nuclear meltdown mode. I remember closing the door to my office and sitting in stunned silence with my office mate and friend. I'd upset people before, but not at this magnitude. The krypton-green minerals began to take hold. I could feel my muscles constricting. I sat on the office couch unable to breath. My first real panic attack. Putting my head between my legs, I felt my whole world spinning; all was vertigo and vestibular chaos.

Whatever Superman-ness I once had was gone.

What An Unhealthy Enneagram 4 Says And Does

I need, I need, I want, I want, gimme gimme gimme.

Ghost their best friend for a week.

Sink in a quagmire of contradictory feelings and emotions.

Yo-yo relationally. Pull people in, push them away, pull people in, push them away.

Go deeper into the basement of shame.

Smile outwardly at their boss while inwardly plotting subterfuge.

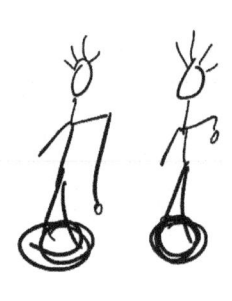

Wallow in self-loathing.

Become an island-dweller, like Tom Hanks in *Cast Away*, who talks to a volleyball.

See-saw back and forth manically from *I'm somebody special*! to *I'm nobody special*!

Sit in the corner at parties, phone scroll, brood, stew, sulk.

Cut off the left ear.

Milk their Holden Caulfield complex of misfitness.

Read Albert Camus's *The Stranger* for the forty-seventh time.

Envy all with a 401(k).

Throw on their college flannel and play Nirvana's song "Lithium" on repeat.

Swear they have lost something, like their keys, passport, or sanity.

Tell happy people to fuck off like Logan Roy.

A Twitter Hunt

It got worse. Come to find out, my boss wanted me to confirm my Twitter posts because he had caught wind of a group of parents who had screenshot the posts and were passing them on to other parents and patrons, starting a nuclear chain reaction of rage and protest. It was the proof they needed to confirm their suspicions about me and the whole woke agenda behind the Interdisciplinary Studies Program. Part of what I have always loved about the school was the boutique-like smallness of it. We didn't operate like Amazon—big, fast, efficient, impersonal. The school was more like the local bookstore down the street where children gather on Saturday mornings for Atticus Finch to read them *Where the Wild Things*. Most of us use the word "family." We call each other by first name, talk about the weather and our kids, and always stop in the cereal aisle in the grocery store and catch up. But there's a shadow side to living in a community that is part *Cheers* and part *Maycomb*. Everyone knows everyone's business and rumors can crash through the community like an asteroid.

What had happened here? I had gone to bed beloved by my school community, like Fred Rogers, and woke up tar-and-feathered, like Colin Kaeperneck. I had heard of cancel culture, even seen cancel culture campaigns on social media against outspoken celebrities, but never in a million years did I think I would be canceled by my own people.

I Googled

So I was curious, and used Google to generate a list of famous people who have struggled with depression. The algorithm spit out a surprising and fascinating list, reinforcing the idea that even superpeople underneath their red capes, big personas, and otherworldly talent are just as exposed, vulnerable, and susceptible to the alien invasion and infection and colonization of depression inside their bodies, brains, and souls.

- Simon Bile
- Jelly Roll
- Jim Carrey
- Lady Gaga
- The Rock
- Jon Hamm
- J.K. Rowling
- Abraham Lincoln
- Prince Harry
- Kristen Bell
- Johnny Deep
- Adele
- The Boss
- Selena Gomez

- Michael Phelps
- Gwyneth Paltrow
- Ryan Renolds
- Beyonce
- Wayne Brady
- Mariah Carey
- Winston Churchill
- Kate Perry
- Michelle Obama
- Liam Payne RIP
- Princess Diana RIP

It Gets Worse

Not long after meeting with my boss about the tweets, I got a random text on my phone. It was from a former student who lived out in Los Angeles.

"I just want you to know that my family and I are with you."

This cryptic text message immediately had my full attention. I pressed him for more information. He told me his family found a pamphlet on Critical Race Theory in their mailbox. It had been circulating in their neighborhood. My Twitter posts had been blown up and printed with my name in big, bold, sinister letters.

The wind suddenly stopped. The air smelled of fish. The roar of a freight train gathered steam. The sky opened, and a spiraling vortex dropped down out of shelf clouds to suck up the earth under my feet.

Things My Oklahoma Brain Says During A Tornado Warning

Prefrontal Cortex: Relax. Statistically speaking, even in a violent tornado, the survival rate is 99%.

Hippocampus: This reminds me of the time when as a kid we jumped into Mom and Dad's eight-foot bathtub—six of us bunched up, knees to chest, with a bed pillow over our heads. Dad had flashlights in both hands, and Mom passed around Chex Mix.

Medial Prefrontal Cortex: Quick! Find a shed and loop your belt to a metal pipe. It worked for Bill Paxton and Helen Hunt in *Twister*!

Ventral Critical Axis: In the name of Jesus, I command you to lift up your demonic tail and go back into the sky!

Amygdala: Fuck me!

Name Death

It was all a blur—a ninja train of time in motion. Trauma has a way of turning our hippocampus into a soupy broth.

There would be a parent petition.

Threats and demands made.

Numbers and tuition dollars crunched.

Emergency Board meetings called.

Bar graphs and pie charts presented.

A Town Hall virtual meeting.

A public apology.

A quiet agreement.

The pound of flesh delivered.

Only then did the hurricane forces relent, revealing the storm's path of destruction.

There's that scene at the end of the play *The Crucible* where John Proctor wrestles with his conscience over whether or not he should confess the sin of witchcraft. I suddenly understood what Proctor meant when he screamed to his detractors:

"Because it is my name! Because I cannot have another in my life!...How may I live without my name? I have given you my soul; leave me my name!"

With two tweets, it felt like my whole body of past work, my reputation, my legacy, and my family's name now hung from the gallows within my school's community.

Illusions

I had taught, college-advised, or coached 70%-ish of the trustees's kids.

I had won a major school award just a year earlier, voted on by my colleagues.

I was good friends with the son of the owner of an NBA franchise and a distinguished alumnus of the school.

The former board chair's son had played basketball for me, and I had helped get him into his dream college.

As far as I knew, no parent of a student of mine had ever filed a formal complaint.

I had helped build the school's robust signature program in college counseling.

I was "the closer" at recruiting events for prospective students and parents.

We all have blind spots. Mine just happened to be the size of a Hummer H2—partly naive, partly egotistical, partly idealistic. I just assumed I had built up enough social capital to make me a kind of Warren Buffet in the school community. Instead, I discovered that in the blink of an eye, I could get shitcanned, joining the Rose family in Schitt's Creek at the Rosebud Motel.

At the end of the day, a private school is a business. Tuition dollars keep the lights on and the school open. With over a million dollars hanging in the balance, I had become a major institutional liability. All with two regrettable tweets. The board had a fiduciary responsibility to protect the school's future from the present. My boss had to represent the board and act in the best interest of the school. Future always first.

Bad Omen

My son was dead wrong. I was damn right. It was an Apache owl for fuck's sake—half-cousin to the raven. I was a doomed vessel. The owl was bad juju all along, an astrological Scorpio in feathers.

In this moment, I now felt like I was wearing the owl like an albatross around my neck—cursed, seasick, dying, killing everyone around me, turning all into poltergeists. It was only a matter of time before I would get shittossed over the side of the boat like Jonah, giving some whale ingestion.

Things Depression Says To An Enneagram 4

Nobody thinks your special, you fucking wannabe magical purple unicorn.

David Rose's melodramatic flair is funny and cute. Yours is not.
Your emotions are too big and loud, like Marty McFly's guitar solo.
Yes, you are as socially awkward as Napoleon Dynamite.

All the world is not a stage, and you're no Leonardo di Caprio as Romeo.
Don't let that call from the past go to voicemail. Pick it up.
Wallow—it suits you, like corduroy.
If you feel invisible in the Starbucks line, it's because you are.

Vincent Van Gogh was an Enneagram 4. Just look at yourself in the mirror, then look at his painting, Self-Portrait with a Bandaged Ear. See? He's your twin with his scraggly red-haired beard and huge, swirling, whirling emotions. He put a bullet in his gut under black skies.

You are not enough.

Reasons Why We Hide From Each Other

Because our

greatgreatgreatgreatgreatgreatgreatgreatgreatgreatgreatgreatgreatgreatgreatgreatgreatgreatgreatgreatgreatgreatgreatgreatgreatgreatgreatgreatgreatgreatgreatgreatgreatgreatgreatgreatgreatgreatgreatgreatgreatgreatgreatgreatgreatgreatgreagreatgreatgreatgreatgreatgreatgreatgreatgreatgreatgreatgreatgreatgreatgreatgreatgreatgreatgreatgreatgreagreatgreatgreatgreatgreatgreatgreatgreatgreatgreatgreatgreatgreatgreatgreatgreatgreatgreatgreatgreatgreagreatgreatgreatgreatgreatgreatgreatgreatgreatgreatgreatgreatgreatgreagreatgreatgreatgreatgreatgreatgreatgreatgreatgreatgreatgreatgreatgreatgreatgreatgreagreatgreatgreatgreatgreatgreatgreatgreatgreatgreatgreatgreatgreatgreagreatgreatgreatgreatgreatgreatgreatgreatgreatgreatgreatgreatgreatgreatgreatgreatgreatgreatgreatgreatgreatgreagreatgreatgreatgreatgreatgreatgreatgreatgreatgreatgreagreatgreatgreatgreatgreatgreatgreatgreatgreatgreatgreatgreatgreatgreatgreagreatgreatgreatgreatgreatgreatgreatgreatgreatgreatgreatgreatgreatgreatgreagreatgreatgreatgreatgreatgreatgreatgreatgreatgreatgreatgreatgreatgreatg reatgreatgreatgreat grandparents did.

I blame them, the motherfuckers.

My Backseat Days

Earlier, I told you how I would sometimes sneak away during my days as the interim MD Director to sit in the front seat of my car, smoke a cigarette, and take a swig of vodka. Wait—what? Just making sure you were paying attention.

That spring, in the wake of the CRT scandal, I took my reptilian-flight-response to another level. I would park my Honda CRV in the faculty parking lot in the morning, wish my son a good day, and then, after he was out of sight, crawl into the backseat, grab the small pillow hidden under the passenger-side seat, and position myself so that the only way anyone could see me was if they directly peered into the tainted windows. Otherwise, only the top of my head and the top of my shoes were visible.

Most days, I set my alarm clock on my phone with just enough time to tuck in my oxford shirt, straighten my tie, and get to a meeting or class. With my phone set, I would put on my earphones, hit the Rain Rain app on my iPhone, and escape into complete unconsciousness. In a 40-hour work week, I probably logged a good 25 of those hours sleeping in the backseat.

I had a few close calls that spring. Seniors in SUVs would sometimes park next to me and see a conspicuous figure in the backseat of my car. Fortunately, no one ever pressed their face against the window to confirm their suspicions. What scared me the most was the thought that someone I loved or cared about would open the door and catch me hiding. At the same time, what scared me was the thought that someone I loved or cared about would not open the door and not find me hiding.

Eucatastrophe

I know now folks in those stories had lots of chances of turning back, only they didn't. They kept going because they were holding on to something. That there's some good in this world, Mr. Frodo, and it's worth fighting for.

—*Sam Wise Gamgee, Two Towers*

Selah

"The divine hears our one-worded prayers," writes Anne Lamott.

Help.

Things That Helped Me During My Dark Days

Pancakes for dinner. Ron Swanson. Sleep. Saying "fuck." Steamy hot showers. Car washes. Sunshine. Fidget toys. Scrolling for teaching jobs in New Zealand. Gathering at the kitchen island for takeout. Eating together. Health checks from friends. Sports talk radio. My prayer beads. Chess. Moon pies. Hitting range balls. Swedish fish. Watching anything other than the news. My son's bare feet. My therapeutic blanket. Long walks. Lunch with my wife. Listening to Sufjan Stevens. Mario Kart Wii with my son. Michigan with Josh Banner. Being around teenagers. Coffee with Graham. Smiling at my students. Drawing doodles. StockX—bidding on Jordans. Dani Rojas.

Breakdownbreakthrough

Holland, Michigan

I had booked a trip months earlier to go up to Michigan in June to spend time with Josh Banner. He lived in Holland, and the tulips would be in late bloom. A couple weeks out, I called Josh and told him I was thinking of not coming. I was in bad shape. There was no way I could show up like this. Josh was adamant.

"Get your ass on the plane."

I warned him. He didn't equivocate. I was getting on Southwest flight 2351 to Grand Rapids.

Josh had built a recording studio and apartment space above his garage. He designed the space to serve as a retreat center for anyone needing a place to rest. One of Josh's superpowers was his hospitality. His care reflected his view of humans as integrated wholes. Josh believed that what affects the psyche also affects the soma. This is because we are embodied souls and ensouled bodies. If something goes wrong in the soul, something goes wrong in the body.

The Greek verb *sozo* was used in Jesus's day to mean both "to save "and "to heal." When Jesus healed someone, he also healed their souls. He worked his holy magic to restore the psychosomatic unity.

Josh didn't lay hands on me like Jesus did with the sick, but he did something just as *sozo-y*. For a week, Josh fed me home cooked-meals and handpicked my local brew. He ground coffee beans from Ethiopia and hand-pressed them for our morning coffee ritual. Each morning, he led me in whole-bodied breathing and centering prayer. Our daily routine would consist of reading, journaling, napping, listening to music, and taking a walk on the beach or in his neighborhood park. Evenings were often casual and chill. We'd make a fire in the backyard fire pit under a canopy of night, light up a cigar, sip bourbon, and simply linger together in the smoke and silence.

Friendship itself can be a form of psychosomatic therapy. For me, Josh offered a space, a rhythm, and an embodiment—a bodysoul presence full of gentleness and compassion.

Showing up in Michigan with nothing, Josh offered me everything.

The Talmud teaches that to save a single life is akin to saving the entire world. If that's true, then Josh saved the whole world because of what he did for me in my greatest need.

The Body And Brain—Part Two

Bessel van der Kolk writes: *The greatest source of suffering are the lies we tell ourselves.*

Most of the lies we tell ourselves wage war within our minds, bodies, and souls.

What we say to ourselves is written and recorded in our bodies.

I had been lying to myself for years. There was a reason for the cellular-level of discomfort inside my body and the psychic amplification of white noise in my head.

I felt and heard it all

because the body keeps the score: the chest tightness, the shortness of breath, the mental exhaustion, the physical exhaustion. The lethargy, as if I were walking through water. The sweat beads around my neck. The lower back spasms.

The brittle toenails. The bad cottonmouth breath. The brain fog the size of the San Francisco Bay. Pulling a Michael Scott and mispronouncing words.

Thoughts of death coupled by thoughts of sex. Insomnia. The need to walk. The need to lie down. The siren voice of a hostess cupcake.

The vestibular disorientation—spinning even while I am standing still. The aching legs. The swollen lymph nodes. Difficulty swallowing. The loss of taste, dead tongued. Numb feet. The ontological sense of floating like a specterballoon. The weightlessness. The extra pounds in the belly region—27 pounds to be exact.

The straitjacket claustrophobia. A future with no future. The deja vu of seeing the same KM cobalt-blue minivan with black rims everywhere I went. Hypochondria. Dark spots forming in the corners of my pupils. Eternal melancholy. Constant body checks for skin cancer. A never-ceasing low hum inside my cochlea.

This foreboding sense that I could drop dead any second, like Ananias. This ominous feeling I was going mad, like the woman who saw broken necks and absurd, unblinking eyes in *The Yellow Wallpaper*. The desire to step out of my skin and disappear into the woods, like the mother in *The Road*.

I'm sorry. No disrespect to those of you who are dualists, but Descartes and Plato were dead fucking wrong.

Hell

When I was in Michigan, there was one particular night I couldn't sleep because my whole body felt like it was on fire. The flames crackled and hissed on my arms, legs, chest, and head. I wanted to scream and jump into a bathtub full of ice; instead, I just thrashed, wiggled, and writhed in bed like a garden snake that had its head chopped off.

I can't remember a time in my life when I didn't believe in hell. As a child, I burned myself while learning how to iron. While my hand bubbled and blistered, my mom told me, *This is what hell would feel like for eternity.* You can imagine me dropping to my knees that very night, with my bandaged hand, praying to God between sobs not to send me on a grease pole to hell.

I'm not sure if I was dehydrated or trapped inside a feverish nightmare. It's very possible that my central nervous system, dysregulated for such a protracted period, simply crashed—like an internal city grid. But I wonder if what I experienced that night was a kind of trauma exorcism.

For years, the trauma had accumulated inside my body like arsenic. Even though I pretended the trauma wasn't there, my body didn't give a flying fuck what I believed or pretended not to believe. My body wanted the trauma demons excised and sent back into the void.

I'm convinced now that it wasn't hell I experienced that night in Holland, Michigan. It was actually a fiery taste of heaven—a kind of neurotheological gesture in which my brain reached out and mercifully extended to my body a kind of holy, healing touch.

Help, Superman, Help!

My dad's genius came out on birthdays. We didn't have money for extravagant parties at Chuck E. Cheese or White Water Bay. We did low-budget parties, all at home with a cake made by mom and streamers from Wal-Mart. Dad was the games coordinator. My favorite game was called *Help, Superman, Help!* The way the game worked was that my dad would yell from somewhere in the house (usually the back closet of the master bedroom), *Help, Superman, Help!* That's when the timer started. Each of us would then take turns, starting in the living room, running through a maze that zigged and zagged its way through the house and backyard. We would have to stop at stations along the way to throw on an oversized T-shirt, size 35-waisted shorts, and size 11 work boots. The last station included a red Superman cape. Throwing on the cape, we would sprint to the final spot, holding our shorts up and trying not to fall out of the giant boots. There, we would find Dad pretending to be locked away by Lex Luthor. Time!

June 2021. A week after my trip to Holland, Michigan.

The garage door groaned open under the heavy Oklahoma heat. A copy of *Frankenstein* stared at me, a stone gargoyle. The sheets of my bed smelled of cold sweat. My head was a swollen cantaloupe. I couldn't lift it to see who was at the bedroom door. A familiar voice tiptoed into the room. It was my father. Again. He was back for part two. In a slow filial cadence, he told me that my wife had called him. Again.

Dad sat on the edge of the bed for a while, then commenced with the same ritual as before.

"Can you describe what you're feeling?"

No response. I looked through him. He was a hologram. Same fucking dance. Just a different fucking song.

The back door opened and shut. I turned my head. It was my youngest brother. That figured. He's the sibling that will drop anything to show up for you. Dad must have sent out a SOS text to the family. I wondered if the family had had a practice drill of some sort, like the drills we have twice a year at the school for a fire, tornado, or active shooter. My brother squeezed me on the shoulder and let out a little groan of sympathy. For a while, we just sat in awkward silence. Normally, I'd offer them bottled water, and we'd shoot the shit about my backyard fescue grass or the OKC Thunder. But I was all blanked out—wordlost, thoughtlost, heartlost, soullost.

Red, snotty, and swollen, I had no fight left in me. I was at the end of myself. My resources were depleted. I knew then that I needed help, like never before in my entire life. There was simply no more rope left, except just enough to hang myself. This shit had to end, one way or the other.

Looking into Dad's eyes, I was suddenly ten years old again. Only this time, it was me calling to him from somewhere in the house, lost and afraid, *Help! Superman! Help!*

Jesus At The Largo

I often think if Jesus were alive today, he'd be doing stand-up comedy at venues like the Largo out in LA. French painter Georges Rouault got it right when he painted Jesus as a clown. Jesus was known for his dark, ironic humor—the kind that only someone with three Long Island iced teas in them could find the comedic genius in. Like the time Jesus told the story of a Palestinian Jew from the West Bank aiding an Israeli Jew by rushing him to the hospital after suffering friendly fire. Or the story of a punk teenager who'd told his dad to drop dead, blew his college money on Vegas strippers and high-stakes Black Jack, only to return home to a black-tie event in his honor. The older I get, the funnier Jesus' jokes get. Perhaps what makes me laugh the hardest are the bits Jesus does that offend religious people. The one thing that gives me hope in all of Jesus' satire and humor is that he truly believes that if God is anywhere on this God-forsaken planet, God is with those who feel God-forsaken.

This Bit Is Called "Blessed"

Blessed are you when you are at the end of your rope.

Blessed are you who contemplate hanging yourself from the ceiling fan with the little rope that's left.

Blessed are you who wonder if God made you on a day she had one too many mojitos.

Blessed are you who ate Honey Buns all week and forgot to shower.

Blessed are you who lay awake all night and doom-shop with your credit card in hand.

Blessed are you who are under the covers and back in Stars Hollow with Rory and Lorelai by four p.m..

Blessed are you who wake up next to your husband strapped into his CPAP machine and fantasize about leaving him for Mark Ruffalo.

Blessed are you who look at yourself in the mirror with an unshaven, slovenly face and icecreambelly and call yourself a disgusting slob.

Blessed are you who fantasize of driving your minivan over a cliff, waving at your kids, husband, and mini schnauzer the whole way down.

Blessed are you who wish someone would take you behind the barn and end it, like Old Yeller.

Good news—the God of the universe is for you and with you and has got your back, no matter how leathery, sun-scorched, and humped over like Richard Nixon.

Magnificent Defeat

For most of my adult life, I have found it hard to ask for help. It feels like weakness—an unattractive quality. The kind that gets you sent home without a rose at the rose ceremony.

I learned a lot about masculinity from Bottomly men, mostly my dad. His name was Roc, a fitting name. He was like a metamorphic rock—strong, durable, unbreakable. Dad went to the Air Force Academy in the 1960s when code red training was legal. He played soccer and tennis there, and was even a squadron squash champion. Dad graduated at the top of his class in aeronautical engineering. He was my childhood hero—bigger, tougher, and more capable than any comic book hero or Brandon Walsh. Dad once got kicked in the head by a horse. Bleeding profusely, he walked over to the minivan and drove himself to the ER as if he was going out to get a half gallon of milk. My granddad, "the Colonel," was even more of a bad-ass. He went to West Point, flew P-32s in the South Pacific, and blasted enemy bogies out of the sky in his F-4 in Vietnam. He was a real-life Maverick. Granddad grew up on the Montana frontier. My favorite story of his as a kid involved a grizzly bear invading his campsite. Granddad snuck out of the tent and ran back home to tell his Pa about the unwelcome visitor. My great-granddad, a Montana Supreme Court Judge, lowered his newspaper and responded, "Well, that's your campsite,

Bo. Go get it back." And that's what my granddad did. He flanked the grizzly bear, pelted the beast with rocks, and screamed "Get out of here, bear!" A bad-ass.

As I sat in the living room with my dad and brother, I began to cry. I was scared and lost—more a child than a man. I was the antithesis of a Bottomly man. There was nothing strong, stoic, or Marvel-heroic about me. I didn't know what to do, where to turn, or how to get beyond my depression. I had come to the end of myself. The existential question hung heavy in the air: *What do I do now?*

The breakdown would be the beginning of a breakthrough.

Little did I know that this would be a moment of magnificent defeat.

If You Can't Change Your Condition

My dad is an actionman. It's his military training. He's like Denzel Washington in *Crimson Tide*—cool and jugular-calm in a nuclear missile crisis. He doesn't panic. Instead, he makes a plan, often on a 3" x 5" index card, and then executes it with the exacting precision of a naval submarine commander.

If we can't change your condition, then we've got to change your situation.

With those words, he sprang into dad-superhero-action. He gathered up my stuff, called my wife, and put me in his car. While I moved into the guest room upstairs at my folks' house, dad reached out to some friends and got the name of a good outpatient clinic in Dallas. He called the clinic and started the process of getting me enrolled. I'd check into the clinic after the holiday break in early July, a couple weeks from now. Dad even called my boss and told him what was happening. My boss had no idea how serious it was. He was ready to help in any way.

You may be wondering: what self-respecting adult man has his dad call his boss for him to ask for a leave of absence? A pathetic one, for sure. And you would be right. Part of coming to the end of yourself is that you are willing to suffer humiliation. The root word for humiliation is *humus* translated "on the ground" or "from the earth." Humiliation, then, is what happens when we have been ground down into dustpowder. We become dirtclods again.

The Brain Is The Body—Part Three

The term "mental illness" can be misleading, as it implies that all the problems happen above the neck. It harkens back to René Descartes and his damn dualism theory. With depression—and with anxiety in particular—a lot of the problems may be generated by the mind, even aggravate the mind, but have physical effects.

For instance, the National Health Society (NHS) website lists these as the mental symptoms of a generalized anxiety disorder:
- Restlessness
- A sense of dread or fear
- Feeling constantly on edge
- Difficulty concentrating
- Irritability

What's fascinating is that the NHS gives as long, if not longer list of physical symptoms:
- Faster, irregular or more noticeable heartbeat
- Feeling lightheaded or dizzy
- Headaches
- Chest paints
- Loss of appetite
- Sweating
- Breathlessness

- Feeling hot
- Shaking

One symptom conspicuously missing from the NHS list is what we will call ontological derealization. This is both a physical and mental symptom in which you feel like a human non-being, a de-ontic alien of some other planetary universe, more wraith-like than fleshy—something thin, stretched, vaporous. It's a total psychosomatic mindfuck because you don't feel fully inside your own skin. You feel like you are controlling the levers of your body from a great distance, somewhere else. It's like the gap between an air traffic controller up in the airport tower and the airplane 50 miles away preparing to land. The cockpit that is you is unoccupied, empty. It is a feeling of the mind and the body, once again proving to the sufferer that to bifurcate the two—as crassly as we do as modern people—is wrong, too simplistic, and reductionist. And maybe part of a bigger problem that we, as modern people, create for ourselves.

Things You Do As A 45-Year Old Depressive Living With Your Parents

Sleep in your own sweat, because it's late June in Oklahoma, and you're upstairs where the heat rises, and your parents keep the air conditioner budgeted at 80 degrees at night.

Sit upstairs and stare out the window at the kids chalking up the sidewalks like a creepy perv.

Pace back and forth across the rickety wood floor panels in your socks, mumbling inchoate.

Sit down for nightly home-cooked dinners at the kitchen table with folded napkins, a patriarchal prayer, and steamy vegetables that taste like 1988.

Watch dad dip his burger in a gob of mayonnaise mixed with barbecue sauce.

Show interest and concern in mom's newest varicose veins.

Listen to your parents try to remember something they've forgotten, like their social security numbers or where they put the ranch dressing in the refrigerator.

Sit on the back porch and talk about the Japanese Maple.

Shower and dry off with a crunchy towel that you're sure you used when you were 12.

Sift through old photographs that mom leaves out for the grandkids. Oh look—the four of us kids in matching floral jams that mom made for us.

Pop in VCR tapes and watch old footage of vacations to Disney World and Bakersfield.

Watch the 9 pm local Fox news and call it a night.

A Conversation With My Son

For the two weeks I lived with my parents, I got a foretaste of what divorced life would be like. The lawyers had brokered an agreement. I'd get a couple hours with my son on the weekend.

A new arcade had opened in the mall. I asked him if he'd like to check it out. He said yes.

On the drive over, there was some initial awkward silence. I finally broke it and asked him how he was doing, how mom and Sully were holding up. His answers were monosyllabic. "Good." I decided to turn on sports talk radio. My son interrupted. I turned the radio off.

"Dad, when are you coming home?"

The question caught me off guard. My son can be a straight shooter. The bullet slug lodged right in between my cavity chest.

"That's a good question. Not exactly sure. Hopefully, at the end of July."

"Mom says you are sick and are going away to get better."

I could feel my jaw tightening.

"Mom's right."

My son glanced over at me and saw my face trembling. He put a hand on my shoulder. He's a very empathetic soul.

"It's okay. Mom and I will be fine. Go get better, dad. I know you can do it."

Goddammit.

"Thank you, bud. I'm going to do my best."

"I know you will, dad."

"I promise."

"I know, dad."

Fucking A.

July 4th

July 4th is America's birthday, a zenith day—full of hotdog contests, barbecues, sparklers, and fireworks.

July 4th, 2021, will go down as one of the low moments in my life—a real nadir point.

It was the eve before I left for Dallas. The outpatient program started on July 6th.

My parents and my siblings invited me to a pool party. I didn't want to go, but they insisted, so I called to see if my son would go with me, this being our last day together for a while. He said sure, as long as we hit up Jake's fireworks stand later.

I've always prided myself on being physically fit. It's part of my vanity, admittedly. Over the past few months, though, I had been in denial about what was happening to my body. I'd avoided eye contact with my naked body in the bathroom mirror. But I'd felt it in my gut, literally and figuratively. At some point, we can't fake out physiological reality. Eating a bowl of Fruit Loops at 10 p.m. in your mid-40s will catch up to you, regardless of your metabolism's hydraulic system. We reap what we sow. Mercy is for the soul. Accountability is for the body.

For almost a year now, I'd stopped doing anything consistently active or physical.

I'd stopped doing 100 push-ups in the morning.

Stopped lifting weights.

Stopped walking the dog on a regular basis.

Stopped taking laps around the school lake.

On my Apple Watch, my daily step count goal had gone from 10,000 steps to 1,000 steps.

My diet had shifted too—fewer veggies, more Twinkies.

Clearly, my metabolism had slowed down, despite my denial and delusions—from a Formula One race car to a coal-driven freight ship.

After arriving at the pool, my son jumped right in and waved me in. I took off my shirt to join him, caught a glimpse of my silhouette reflected in the pool water and recoiled in horror. I was wearing my depression like an inflatable sumo wrestling suit. My arms were pink and flabby, my face and jowls swollen. And worst of all, I had man boobs, cone-shaped, big enough to fit in a D-cup bra. If I would have shown René Descartes a before-and-after picture of my physical body—pre-depression and in-depression—I am fairly confident he would have tossed his whole mind-body dualism theory into the deep end of the pool. Here was verifiable proof that what happens in our brains affects our bodies; the darkly invisible becomes grotesquely visible. Head depression equals body inflation.

I immediately put back on my shirt, waved off my son, and pulled my pool chair as far away from everyone as possible, hiding my embarrassed eyes behind dark sunglasses. I would sit this one out. Of course, a couple hours later, when dad asked me how many burgers he should grill up for me, I told him two, maybe four.

D-Town

A pebble-size crack caught my eye. It was on the brink of spinning a gnarly web across my windshield. I'd put 150,000-plus miles on my Honda CRV and never noticed it. Often seen is no longer seen, says Gandalf. It always starts small—a questioning question, a furled brow of incredulity, a pushback here, a pushback there. And then it veins out through the never-ending siege of spiraling discussion, debate, demands, and deadlines. The psyche absorbs it all, spongy, like an amoeba.

Malcolm Gladwell's theory on airplane crashes is full of irony, yet makes sense. It's never one big dramatic thing, like engine failure, or a wing ripping off, or a pilot going into cardiac arrest. It's small issues and malfunctions and errors—often a combination of things that go awry with the plane and the pilot's judgment—that cause the plane to crash.

Gladwell's airplane crash theory couple apply to depression. Even though it may feel like the psychosomatic crash has one major cause, like a pandemic, petition, or painful resignation, it's often the little micro-stressors, micro-emotions, and micro-cognitive dissonances that cause the body-brain machinery to malfunction and lead to personal choices that inevitably result in an emotional crash.

A sign post read: Dallas 120 miles.

In the past, I'd always liked going down to Dallas. I spent some of my childhood there.

A memory bubbled up. I'm 5 years old again; it's Sunday afternoon, autumn. With my Dallas Cowboy hat strapped on and shirtless, I jump up into my dad's lap and curl into his chest, ready to cheer on Danny White and Tony Dorsett.

Dad's voice startled me out of my reverie. He asked me if I wanted to pull off around Denton to grab dinner before we check into the hotel. I nodded, maybe Chick-fil-A. The website said the three-week, out-patient program would include daily devotions, group sessions, art therapy, and individual counseling sessions. Daily devotions—*a slight wince*. I pictured Jesus in a red cardigan and blue boat shoes, warm and reassuring like Mr. Rogers. Group sessions. I'd only seen those on TV, like Jesse's character in *Breaking Bad*. I rehearsed my introduction.

Hi, my name is Josh. When I was born, my dad wanted to name me Bear Bottomly. That's no joke. My mom intervened. Thank God. Let's see. I am married and have a teenage son. I'm a defrocked administrator—so there is that. As far as hobbies, I like to play golf, drink coffee, and walk my dog. Oh yeah, and I am here because I wake up every morning and want to die.

First drafts are always shitty, writes Anne Lamott. I'll rehearse again later.

I stared out the window for the longest time, the highway asphalt a greasy shine under the sun's rays. Dad put on the blinker and pulled into the hotel. The clinic facility was down the street, within walking distance.

I only brought my Birkenstocks; my feet will get sweaty walking back and forth. I should probably clip my toenails.

Check In

Our hotel was just up the street. Dad walked with me to the clinic. Silence accompanied us in the space between.

He sat next to me while I did paperwork with one of his four-colored Bic pens. Dad always placed his Bic pen on his dresser next to his wallet and pocket-size appointment book on his dresser. As a kid, I used to grab the pen from his dresser and play with it, clicking each color with my curious thumbs. I clicked the black ink, more formal. Afterward, an older woman appeared in the door, smiled, and motioned for me to join her. She felt safe, grandmotherly. I nodded, strapped on my backpack, and followed her. I glanced back and forced a smile. I could tell Dad wanted to hug me, or kiss me, or fold me into his lap like he did on Sundays during football season.

"3 p.m.," he said. "I'll meet you here and walk back to the hotel with you."

He's always been a good father.

Testing

Standardized tests trigger me. I've never been a good test taker. In high school, I took the ACT five times. I blame my parents. No child should have to get up at 7:00 a.m. on five separate Saturdays to fill in electronic bubbles for five hours. It's child abuse. Someone should have called DHS on them.

The first official thing I was asked to do was complete the Minnesota Multiphasic Personality Inventory (MMPI-2), a written psychological assessment used to diagnose mental disorders—the equivalent of the SAT for mental illness. All 338 questions were true or false. I was told it would take 25-30 minutes to complete the five-page test manual. A little over an hour, I was on question 224. My brain still didn't work *good*. Or was it work *well*? I moved through each question and section slowly and effortfully, like I was driving in fog on a curvy, hilly road with 20/80 vision.

Some questions felt like ice breakers, nothing to do with mental health.

I like mechanics magazines. False. I can't even change the oil.

I would like to be a singer. True—something between Bono and Adam Levine.

I enjoy detective or mystery novels. True for the former—anything by Michael Connelly.

Other questions invoked memories.

At times, I have very much wanted to leave home. True-ish if we're talking about childhood. Once, when I was ten, I packed a duffle bag and walked out. Not sure why. Maybe I was protesting the 30-minutes-a-day TV rule. I got all the way down my street, en route to Eric Morris's house, and turned around. My bluff was called. I was hungry for mom's lasagna.

I have never been in trouble with sexual behavior. True. I didn't know what masturbation was until I was 18. I'm. Not. Shitting. You. That's how much of a purity culture bubble I lived in—it was like *The Truman Show* for virgins.

I do many things that I regret afterwards. True. Every time I have masturbated since I was 18.

Some questions probed my character.

I do not always tell the truth. If I say False, I'd be lying. It's true that I've inherited my granddad's proclivity for magical realism.

I like to tease animals. No—except that one time as a kid with a cat. I'm still ashamed.

I like being around people. False (most of the time). Larry David put it succinctly on *Curb Your Enthusiasm*: "I think I'm doing pretty good at this party, considering I don't like people."

And then there were the "let's-get-down-into-your-shit" questions.

I wake up fresh and rested most mornings. False. I wake up most mornings and Google cryogenic freezing or cryo sleeping.

At times, I feel like swearing. True. Is there a diagnosis called manic depressive Tourette syndrome? If so, I've got it in spades! *doublefucksdoublefucksdoublefucks*

At times, I have the urge to do something harmful or shocking. Does shaving my head and getting a face tattoo like Mike Tyson count?

I did have my favorite questions.

At times, I feel like becoming invisible. True. If I had the One Ring, I would put it on and never take it off again until I turned into Gollum.

At times, I have a low sex drive. That's not a simple question. I have increased sexual fantasies but a decreased sexual appetite. Is there such a thing as hyper-erectiontivity of the imagination while simultaneously suffering from erectile dysfunction? If not, I might make for an interesting case study.

At times, I want to smash things. True. I have Hulk-like moments where I want to transmogrify into a ripped, muscular green man and smash up cars and tanks and white supremacist.

After I finished the assessment, I put down my number 2 pencil and immediately wondered if I passed, not really knowing what "passed" means. The last assessment I took of this magnitude were my written and oral exams for my master's degree. I knew what passing meant in that context—the ability to explain gestalt theory, metaphysical poetry, Vietnam War literature and existential philosophy, mythopoeia in Tolkien's fantasy. With this assessment, I was left feeling naked, exposed, uncertain, more wobbly than sturdy, and convinced I would have a major vulnerability hangover the next day. But at the same time, I was tired of the constant PR spin.

Oscar Wilde said it best: *The truth is rarely pure and never simple.*

I knew that if I wanted to bend the arc of my mental health in a new trajectory, I had to get down into the messy, ugly, dirt-cloddy, nauseous, vomity, fuck-awful truth within myself.

The way to health was to face the truth of the lies I had been telling myself and others around me for a loonnnnnggggg ass time. Which really sucks. No two ways around that R-rated truth.

Group Therapy

Twice a day in the program, I had group therapy led by one of the clinic's counselors. This was a new experience for me. I was as curious as I was skeptical.

Our first session was a chance to meet each other, say a little bit about ourselves. I had refined my shitty draft, shortened it. As each person took turns sharing, I noted the diversity in the room; we were very *Breakfast Club*-ish. There was a dentist from Arkansas who liked to fish and hunt. A tall blonde in her mid-twenties sporting lululemon leggings, a college volleyball coach. A middle-aged woman with three adult children, always knitting a scarf during our sessions. A businessman who drove a Porsche and talked on his phone between sessions. A college student with purple streaks in her hair. A high school dropout from Louisiana with a mullet. A rising college freshman in a polo shirt and khaki shorts, a lacrosse player. And me, a middle-aged teacher from Oklahoma in Birkenstocks (with socks).

Part of our introduction had to include why we were in the program. Each person's reasons confirmed what I knew but still hadn't really believed. Even though we all came from different walks of life, different parts of the country, with different hair cuts, and different jobs, we were actually not all that different. Each of us was in the program because we had bottomed out. At some point, we had all come to the end of our own resources. Not surprisingly, we all had something in the recent past that had pushed us over the edge: a spouse who cheated, a husband who asked for a divorce, an abusive boyfriend, a close friend who committed suicide, a recent poor job review, a report card with a B-, a recruiting process that ended with no D1 scholarship offers, and a middle-aged guy who shouldn't post on social media.

I had been in groups before—book clubs, men's groups, Bible studies. In those groups, we talked about things, sometimes about ourselves. But we never talked about what was going on inside of ourselves. That was something I had only begun to do with a therapist. And on occasion with my best friend.

Over time in those group sessions, I began to understand why organizations like A.A. have 80 years of proven success. There is real power when we gather with people who share a similar struggle and ache. In that shared space, it was safe to take off the rigid armor. We could go off-brand. What I loved most was that we got regular practice at being fully present, actively listening to each other, learning to honor each other's voice, and giving each other full permission to be vulnerable and courageous. We gave no advice. We offered no fix. We answered no questions. As you can imagine, as we practiced presence-centered listening, we all found it easier and easier to extend to each other empathy and compassion. Countless times, as I listened to my peers, I found myself saying, me too. Those two words have nuclear power. They can light up the whole city grid inside of us. When we discover that someone else has thought those dark thoughts, felt those painful feelings, or done those strange things, we no longer feel as alone, as alien, as other. Instead, we feel a sense of connection, a sense of being seen and valued, a part of something instead of apart from something.

In those group sessions, more than anything, I felt something even more powerful than human being-ness. I felt human belonging-ness.

Belonging

Here's the deal. We all live inside the petri dish of this beautifully strange and strangely beautiful planet. Whether you wear designer jeans or camouflage crocs, drive a Ford truck or rent a Lime scooter, believe in a higher deity or don't, watch Fox News or CNN, listen to *Armchair Experts* or Joe Rogan, have an honors-roll kid or high school dropout, live in LA or live in OKC—it doesn't matter. We're all susceptible to struggles with mental health. Depression shows no favoritism. Many of the greatest and, well, toughest people of all time have suffered from depression. Ernest Hermingway pulled a shotgun on himself to end his long battle with depression. Dr. King wrote openly about the times he felt like he couldn't go on in the Civil Rights movement. Mother Teresa wrote candidly about her struggles with atheistic despair. Michael Phelps tells his story of mental illness in a documentary. Billie Eilish recently opened up about her struggle with suicidal ideation. Dax Prescott brought awareness to the NFL community when he talked about his mental health challenges in the aftermath of his brother's suicide. Even Taylor Swift dedicated a song on her *Tortured Poets Department*

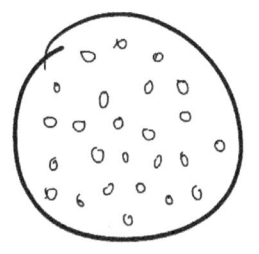

album to lament the charade of stardom to cover up her own depression.

You and I are no less or more of a man or a woman or human for having depression than you would be for having diabetes, getting cancer, or developing a yip in your golf swing.

The point is that depression and mental health is something that either touches us or touches someone close to us. We're all in the soup together.

So what's the answer? How do we respond to this dilemma?

It's not rocket science. Though it is certainly documented in social science. It's what my dad and brother did for me in the living room. It's what I experienced in group therapy. It's what my therapist and I did weekly after I returned from treatment. It's what I still do today on Marco Polo regularly with my best friend.

Talk.

Listen.

Encourage talking.

Foster listening.

Create a safe space for mutual vulnerability where the mirror neurons can bond together.

Add new layers to the conversation.

Keep a vigilant eye out for those wanting to join in the conversation.

Reiterate again and again that depression is not something you admit to like a porn addiction or laundering money for the Kansas City mob. Nor is it something you blanch about in embarrassment; it is a human experience. Regardless of age, gender, ethnicity, sexual orientation, level of education, voter registration, income bracket, vaccination record, religious preference, or favorite sports team. It is not you. It is simply something that happens to you. And something that can be eased by talking—words, comfort, care, support. It took me having a mental breakdown in my son's twin bed on the day we celebrated the Resurrection Man to be able to talk openly, even with my closest friends and family, let alone anyone else, about my experience. I've since discovered that the very act of talking with someone about mental health is a kind of therapy. The conversation has curative powers. Where there is talk, there is healing. And where there is healing, there is hope.

Test Results Day

One afternoon, I was pulled out of group therapy and escorted back to a corner office with a Ph.D.-ed name on the door sign. I was greeted by a woman with her hair pulled back, wearing black slacks and a tan blouse—all business. She held a vanilla folder with my name on it. My legs suddenly locked, like my dog entering the vet examination room. The flinty look on her face made me think there was a CT scan of stage four cancer inside the folder.

She invited me to sit and said we would go over the MMPI-2 results. Her voice and inflection was flat— emotionless. As she opened the folder, I could feel the straddling activity in my brain— half in my prefrontal cortex, half in my amygdala.

Usually, when I go over a poor test with one of my students, I'll lead with the positive and touch on what the student did well on the assessment. Celebrate the wins. Lower the cortisol levels. Get my students out of their Godzilla brain. Once they are relaxed and engaged in their frontal lobe, then I hit them with the red ink stuff.

This Ph.D. woman pulled me right under like a great white shark.

- *Depression T > 75: Serious clinical depression; suicidal ideation; feelings of unworthiness and inadequacy.*
  All spot on, especially the last one. Effing breasticles.

- *Psychasthenia T > 75: Extreme psychological turmoil (i.e. fear, anxiety tension, depression); intruding thoughts, unable to concentrate; obsessive-compulsive symptoms.*
  That tracks and helps explain my neurotic compulsion to check my email Inbox 300 times a day to read, file, or delete my way to 0 emails. My wife's Inbox has 24,546 unread emails. Even a glimpse of her Inbox turns me into a werewolf.

- *Schizophrenia T = 55-64: Limited interest in other people; impractical; prone to fantasy and daydreaming; feelings of inadequacy and insecurity.*
  Pretty spot on. Most days, I feel generally annoyed by everyone, especially people who teeth-smile.

- *Hypomania T = 55-64: Prone to purposeless activity; confusion; flights of ideas; lacks direction; conceptual disorganization; unrealistic self-appraisal; impulsive, low frustration tolerance.*

That last one might explain why I am prone to going "Happy Gilmore" on the links—throwing clubs, cursing golf balls, and, on occasion, snapping a club's titanium neck over my knee.

- *Social Introduction T > 65-74: Introverted; depressed; guilty; slow to personal tempo; lacks self-confidence; lacks interest; submissive; compliant, emotionally over-controlled.*
  All true. I have no spine, no voice. I'm a robotic host and concierge, like Ted Flood in *Westworld*—only without the chaps, cowboy boots, and sex appeal.

When the Ph.D. woman finished the results review, she had me sign something, like an NDA or my adult consent to a lobotomy.

I've walked out of many offices in my life: principal's offices, doctor's offices, professor's offices, coach's offices, therapist's offices, dean's offices, boss's offices, even a donor's office. But that office visit felt like I had entered Dante's Inferno—abandon all hope, ye who enter.

Some progressive theologians and biblical scholars argue that hell is not a postmortem physical reality, not an actual place like El

Paso, Texas. Hell is instead a state of mind, a postmortem mental prison locked from the inside. Who really knows? All I knew as I walked out of that Ph.D.'s office was that I was a standard deviation or two beyond healthy, beyond flourishing, beyond heaven. If indeed I was in my own hell, a prison of my own creation, then I had to summon the courage to attempt an escape, like Andy Defresne.

The 1 Percent Rule

For the longest time, *Atomic Habits* sat on my lamp stand staring at me from under the ambient light. I had no mental energy to read; the power switch was off. Then one day, I mustered enough strength to open Clear's book and read Lesson 1: Small Habits Make a Big Difference. What resonated immediately was Clear's theory of the 1% rule. It went something like this: If you can get 1 percent better each day for one year, you'll end up thirty-seven times better by the time you're done. Conversely, if you get 1 percent worse each day for one year, you'll decline nearly down to zero.

The math didn't make total sense—math never did to me. But the theory did make sense. Once in college, I suffered a shooting slump. After practice, the assistant coach pulled me aside and had me do a form-shooting drill with him. I stood right in front of the basketball goal, three feet away, and practiced the same one-handed shot over and over again. I had to follow and recite out loud each time three simple steps: 1) Square the shoulders, 2) Elbow in, and 3) Follow through.

Every day, before and after practice, I did the same drill, the same routine, and the same three steps. When I first started, I thought my coach was nuts. This was some wax-on, wax-off bullshit. But guess what? My shooting percentage improved, to the point that, by the season's end, I was leading the team in three-point shooting percentage. My assistant coach was a mad genius after all—like Mister Miyagi.

When I checked into the clinic, I had to complete a medical exam, which, unfortunately, included stepping on a scale. That alone was motivation.

So, I gave Clear's 1% rule a try.

Every morning, I started my day by doing push-ups, just five push-ups—honestly, was all I could manage. My goal was 100 consecutive push-ups by January 1st. That gave me almost five months to get there. I figured most people use the new year to set exercise goals; I wanted to meet my goals on that holiday.

And so, I began to do my atomistic exercise, my 1% of five push-ups a day. Over time, five became ten. Then fifteen. By October, forty. By November, fifty. By December, seventy-five. And on January 1st—one fucking hundred!

In his book *The Tools*, psychiatrist Dr. Phil Stutz says that your relationship to your physical body impacts how you feel. In fact, Stutz argues that 85% of mental health comes down to sleep, nutrition, and exercise.

I believe Stutz more than ever.

Human bodies are made up of tissue, bone, and muscle. Break that down and we're made up of molecules and cells. Break that down further, and we're made up of billions upon billions of atoms. The point is: we shouldn't be surprised that we evolve and grow through atomic-sized changes to habits and behaviors. It's baked into the whole shebang—bodies, stones, animals, trees and stars.

The key then in habit formation involves breaking things down to their simplest and smallest parts.

Whatever the habit—doing push-ups, running a mile, taking up yoga, eating more vegetables, watching less porn, taking longer walks, practicing gratitude, reading a book, praying.

So, how do you get started?

Well, again, I don't think it is astrophysics. It was never meant to be that complicated. The answer is as simple and as small as an atom and particle.

Just start.

Tough Love

Growing up, my dad was prone to push us four kids to do things that we didn't always want to do. Not extreme things, like reading the book of *Leviticus* or post-nuclear apocalyptic survival training—just nudge us to levels of discomfort, angst, and ughness.

Growing up in Colorado Springs, Dad was notorious for bait-and-switching us when it came to family hikes. As we loaded up in the minivan, he'd promise a leisurely nature walk. Before we knew it, we were three miles up on a six-mile loop, our legs burning from switchbacks on trailheads lined with loose soils and rocks. Once, in high school, Dad made me hike down the Grand Canyon when I wasn't feeling well. I later tested positive for strep throat and impetigo.

On my road to mental health recovery, Dad often showed me tough love—a microcosm of how he parented me in my formative years. While staying with me during my time in the Dallas clinic, Dad would push me to do things I didn't want to do in my depressed, low energy state—like taking walks, playing golf, or getting me up for a hearty breakfast before my first group session at 8 a.m.

After most days in the program, Dad would let me swap out my Birkenstocks for my Nike Zooms and take me over to this heavily wooded area near Highland Park. We'd walk a trail that meandered along a creek bed below. He'd say, "Let's just walk for ten minutes or so."

I knew that trick. But I pretended to fall for it every time.

Ten minutes turned into twenty. Into thirty. Into an hour.

Most days when we'd walk, I wouldn't say anything—just keep my head down, processing the day's therapeutic work and keeping an eye out for snakes. Dad always respected my need for space, silence, and snake watching.

Here's the hard truth: Getting well isn't for the faint of heart. It's a fucking grind.

And, yes, there will be moments when you will want to ring the bell and call it quits.

That's when you need a drill sergeant more than a therapist or psychiatrist. Not one to run you out of the mental health program, but one to keep you in it.

Dad was that Navy SEAL-like drill sergeant for me. He made me do things I didn't want to do then so that I could enjoy everything again now.

Thank you, Dad. I owe much of my full recovery to you and your tough love.

Arts And Crafts And Steph Curry

One of our program assignments involved arts and crafts. The project had three parts. Part one was to draw a picture or create a collage of how we think others see us. Part two involved drawing a picture or creating a collage of how we see ourselves. Part three focused on how we want to see ourselves.

Our counselor pointed to a huge stash of magazines on a table next to scissors (only brought out under close monitoring for the activity), glue, and poster board. For a long while, I sat and pondered, brainstorming and striking the pose of Auguste Rodin's *The Thinker*. Finally, I settled on making a collage for part one and drawing something for parts two and three. Then, I went to work.

Part One: How I Think Others See

I cut out a picture of Stephen Curry. I am perceived as part athlete.

I cut out a photo of Justin Timberlake. I am seen as part entertainer—and (*was*—past tense) a good dancer.

I cut out a gorgeous photo of an aspen enclave in the golden thrush of autumn. I am seen as a naturalist and romanticist, a contemplative mystic.

I cut out a picture of Colson Whitehead's Pulitzer-winning novel *The Nickel Boys.* I am perceived as a reader, writer, creative, subversive, and deep thinker.

I cut out a picture of a miniature Goldendoodle. They say you can tell a lot about someone's personality by the kind of dog they have. I am the proud, longtime, and loving owner of a Cavapoo—a mix of King Cavalier and Poodle. My dog is small-ish at 39 pounds, neutered, hypoallergenic, a lap dog when in the mood. He barks a big game at bigger dogs and Amazon workers but cowers at the sound of thunder or the blender.

The first part of arts and crafts was easy because I had spent prodigious amounts of time and energy thinking, fretting, and worrying about what others think of me. It's what Enneagram 4s do naturally when healthy but obsessively when unhealthy and in a boxing match with their shadow selves.

When I presented to the group, I felt like I was doing stand-up, turning every piece of my collage into a comedy bit of self-effacing humor. The audience laughed through my whole riff. I was on fire—like John Mulaney.

Part Two: How I See Myself

In the hero's journey, the most terrifying moment for the protagonist is the descent into a kind of cave to confront their shadow self—their deepest fears. The most famous example is in *Empire Strikes Back* when Luke Skywalker must enter the Cave of Evil as part of his Jedi training by Yoda. As Luke steps down into the cave, he feels something cold and menacing grip him. Then, he sees Darth Vader. Red and blue lightsabers light up the cave; they duel, and upon gaining the upper hand, Luke beheads Darth Vader. But behind the dark mask, he sees an image of himself. Luke realizes a Darth Vader-self lives within his own blood and bones. He must face the truth that what he fears most is himself.

When I closed my eyes and turned inward, descending down into my own inner cave, I saw an image of myself I didn't want to admit was there. I saw something small, diminutive—more child than adult, more boy than man, more Frodo than Aragorn. I saw something that couldn't protect himself, let alone others.

I saw my elementary school self, sitting in the front of the bus, hunched over, holding hands with my little sister, praying to God that Jim, the grizzled old bus driver that smelled like aged cheese, wouldn't pull over because of the shenanigans going on in the back of the bus, forcing us to walk home.

I saw my middle school self—scrawny, all bony arms and knobby legs, barely able to lift the 45-pound weight bar for bench press—the laughingstock of the football team.

I saw my high school self—the one my classmates called a religious fraud and "huckstucker," a Jesus-monster.

I saw my college self—an utter disappointment and a bust of a recruit on the basketball court, a terrible draft pick.

I saw a version of myself as an adult: impotent, infertile, a failed progenitor—a blank shooter. I saw a man who was a parody of his own father, a sad mockery of his own flesh and blood.

Simply put, I saw something who was never going to be enough.

When I shared my drawing with the group, I felt this low-level nausea scraping along my stomach—a kind of shame-sickness. None of my running commentary was funny or enjoyable to talk about openly. It was painful, acid-like. Yet, I felt something strange and nascent forming—a pattern.

I felt it during group time. I felt it during one-on-one sessions with my therapist. I felt it when I journaled. I felt it standing near the coffee machine while in conversation with the dentist from Arkansas. It's hard to articulate because it involved a simultaneous phenomenon—a paradox. I felt both hurting and healing at the same time. It was like the deeper the wound, the more painful the healing.

Part Three: How I Want to See Myself

This was the hardest part. If only I could draw a picture of Bradley Cooper or Travis Kelsey and be done with it. Unfortunately, this exercise required far more challenging: to see beyond the walls of despair. I had to stretch my imagination northward—to scan the galaxies of possibility and discover my future self, my more cosmic self.

This was a self who had experienced a kind of transcendence. A self healed from past pain and trauma. A self no longer operating from fear or anxiety. A self who had rediscovered the sound of his own voice—strong and vibrant and powerful, like a lion. A self who had returned from exile, finding home again inside his own skin, living freely, courageously, and wildly from his heart.

I doodled a figure inside a galaxy of circles. Each circle was distinct yet connected and integrated into the others—a kind of unity in diversity, a kind of dance. In this picture, I captured a feeling of oneness within myself and everything else. I imagined a self that was whole, authentic, and centered, capable of moving through the universe of interconnected relationships free to love, laugh, weep, dance, and live into my deepest parts of my being.

When I presented this picture to the group, I could feel light and warmth and music inside my breath, lungs, and limbs. For a moment, amidst the lyrical melody of my words, I caught a glimpse beyond the walls of this world—a fleeting vision of my future self. This was a self who had recovered the most precious of gifts: the gift of joy. A joy that one can only find on the other side of grief and despair.

Eucatastrophe occurs when we pass through something that forces us to face the pain, trauma, and despair inside our own minds, bodies, and souls. The calamity we endure is not punitive, though it can feel that way. Instead, it awakens something again inside of us—something long dormant under a dark spell, something that makes us more fully alive and human.

In the hero's journey, the cave paradoxically becomes a womb for rebirth. Within the darkness of the cave, the protagonist has a revelation—a burst of light within the conscious mind that breaks the spell. Upon emerging, they have undergone a transformation—a rebirth of consciousness and character. The dual self—the false self, or the self at war with itself—has been defeated. What emerges from the cave is the unified self, the authentic self, whole and integrated.

During my last presentation to the group, I didn't experience any kind of radical rebirth of consciousness. Far from it. If anything, I experienced a fleeting glimpse of a possible future beyond my current depressive state. But in that moment, I felt something akin to real hope—a bright bird that flew into my drab little heart-cage, flapped its bright feathers, and sang in a lyrical voice.

Final Exam

The program's final exam involved writing out a version of our life story to share with the group. The goal was twofold: (1) to connect the dots to the major themes in our story and (2) to face our story with bravery, owning all its parts—the tragedy, comedy, and fairy tale.

What I found fascinating in the writing process was what bubbled up to the surface. Memories have a mind of their own, don't they? I thought I knew what I wanted to write, but as I began, it was almost like an invisible hand reached in and guided my pen. I became less an author and more a stenographer.

Here's what I wrote and shared with the group:

Writing is really quite simple; all you have to do is sit down at your typewriter and open a vein—another hematological image. From the writer's vein into the reader's vein: for better or worse a transfusion…For my money anyway, the only books worth reading are books written in blood.
—Frederick Beuchner

This is my attempt to open a vein and tell you my story in my own blood.

When I zoom out and look at the 'Google Earth map' of my life's geography, I see a landscape defined by two different types of terrain: one part is severe, brown and scorched; the other part is gentle, green, and lush. This is the topography of my life's journey. This is the leitmotif of my story—a repeated pattern of eucatastrophe, of good calamity.

In 9th grade, we moved to Colorado Springs for my dad's job. I was devastated. Oklahoma was my home, full of friends, a school, a girl I liked, an amazing basketball coach, and a college team I loved to root for (OU Sooners). A year later, though, I had new friends, a girlfriend, a great basketball coach, and a new college team to root for (CU Buffs).

In 10th grade, I suffered a knee injury and regressed as a basketball player, losing my starting position. Discouraged, I decided not to play my junior year. The first practice came and went. Dad told me to give basketball another try. I did. And the rest is history. We went on to win the school's first state championship, and I would even hit a last-second shot in the state quarterfinal—the kind of shot I practiced as a kid in the backyard. It was a dream come true.

In college as a player, I suffered a back injury, one I'd never completely heal from. I decided to retire and transfer colleges. A year later, I was a volunteer assistant coach at a local high school. Two years later, I was named the head varsity basketball coach at that same school. And in my third year as head coach, our team won the 2A state championship.

In college, I met a girl, fell in love, and eventually got engaged. For reasons I still don't fully understand, we couldn't set a wedding date. We dragged our feet over a year, finally breaking up—both of us heartbroken. Two years later, I met a girl from Iowa. She looked like Winnie Cooper from *The Wonder Year*. I was instantly thunderstruck. My childhood TV crush had become an adult reality! There was a God after all! Winnie and I were married six months later to Kevin Arnold's dismay.

I thought I would teach and coach at the school I started at forever. But a new athletic director came in and ran me off from coaching. That painful ordeal led me to apply for a job at another school. I was hired, and am now in my 20th year there.

Five years ago, I was promoted to Associate Head of Academics. At the time, I thought I would enjoy the transition from the classroom as a teacher to an administrator in an office. I was wrong. This past spring, I was pulled into the vortex of a CRT controversy over something I posted on social media. I'll spare you the regrettable details, but that abyss experience brought me here—ashamed, exhausted, burned out, disillusioned, cynical, and suicidal.

In closing, I am fighting for the good, not knowing what that goodness will look like. I am holding on to faith that this eucatastrophic pattern of calamity first and good second will once again prove true in my life's story, and that I will make a full recovery of my health and happiness.

Some years for our anniversary, my wife and I uncork a glass of wine and toast the year behind us and the year ahead. As we sip down our memories and hopes, we say to each other, The best is yet to come.

I choose to believe this for my journey ahead, even though I don't see it or feel it.

The best is yet to come.

Selah

"The divine hears our one-worded prayers," writes Anne Lamott.

Thanks.

Things I Gave Thanks For During The Dark Days

My wife's smart, self-effacing humor. My son's ironic, dry humor. Diet Dr. Peppers. *Armchair Expert*. 18 holes of golf with Dad during twilight rates. My psychiatrist. My students and their laughter. Weekend naps. Roy Kent. Clean public bathroom stalls. My siblings—their text messages, memes, emojis. My dog's daily greeting at the garage door. Chick-fil-A. Pickleball. The backyard greenbelt and the red cardinals. Lululemon underwear. The Dunder Mifflin basketball game episode of *The Office*. Tuesday afternoons with my therapist. My office mate. Braum's ice cream. *Bridgerton*. The Battle at Helm's Deep. Mitch Park. Brene Brown. Bluebird Books. Rob Bell. My mother-in-law's beef stroganoff. Whitney's cards with poems. Reese Witherspoon and Vince Vaughn in *Four Christmases* ("Mistletoe!"). The minute after I turn off the bedside lamp.

The Corkscrew Effect

Upon graduating from the program and returning home, I agreed to meet with my therapist once a week. That was a non-negotiable. As he and I resumed our sessions again, we spent a lot of time discussing the road to full recovery. My therapist told me about the myth of linear progress. We often think that recovery should follow a clean, straight, upward trajectory—moving neatly along a north-bound y-axis. But as he repeatedly emphasized, that's unrealistic and not how recovery works. Instead of a straight line, we should expect a corkscrew process.

Later, my therapist later emailed me and elaborated on the corkscrew process:

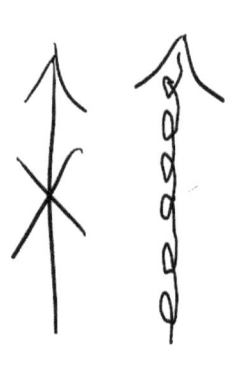

The premise of the corkscrew effect is progress is not a linear process (despite what we are taught or would like it to be). A major flaw of the linear model is that relapses or slip-ups typically mean going back to the beginning and/or starting over. This creates a fear of failure and invalidates our progress when setbacks inevitably occur. The linear model assumes we have it all figured out and can simply follow through, but this notion eventually fails.

In contrast, the corkscrew effect illustrates progress as a process of trial and error—practice and refinement—as we discover what works and what else is needed for growth and development. The corkscrew model accepts that relapses and mistakes are inevitable, even essential, to progress. While setbacks can be painful, they also provide opportunities to learn. Moreover, the corkscrew effect depicts relapses as a loop, allowing us to pick up where we left off. There's no starting over because no one can erase the progress we've already made.

How liberating was my therapist's explanation? For me, it perfectly described my own journey of growth and recovery. I would make progress for a few days, only to have depression reappear and pull me back. At those times, I'd return to my therapist's office, frustrated that the damned corkscrew had gotten the better of me again. Together, we would work through my shame, analyzing my habits, choices, and behaviors that shaped my mental health. Two lists emerged from our discussions: of things to avoid and another of things to embrace. The former only made the corkscrew worse, while the latter helped me rise above its twists.

My therapist would often say two things to me:

- "We name things to tame things." In this case, to unscrew things.
- "We name things to manifest things," especially the small, luminous balls of energy that contain hope, health, and light.

Things To Avoid

- Doom Scrolling
- McDonald's double cheeseburgers with large fries
- Political idealogues
- Prosperity gospel theology
- Religious triumphalism
- Less than six hours of sleep
- Naps lasting longer than an hour
- Mid-afternoon coffee
- Spiraling thoughts in the dark
- Doing the laundry without permission
- Holocaust movies
- Gotham City
- Sitting at my desk too long
- Slouching in my chair
- Attempting DIY house repairs
- Reading more than 10 emails at once
- Grading more than 5 papers at a time
- Extended separation from loved ones
- Telling a lie
- Leaving a bad tip
- Hiding a new pair of shoes
- Playing slot machines with my debit card handy
- Obsessing over my son's future

- Checking my 403b balance
- Neglecting to walk the dog
- Scorching hot days
- Skipping weightlifting for a week
- Missing a day of centering prayer
- Overconsuming or overposting on social media
- Spreadsheets on student absences
- Sedentary days sinking into the couch
- Porn
- Reading bumper stickers on trucks
- Flying and airports
- Inadequate hydration
- Watching the local news
- Frosted covered donuts with sprinkles
- Anything by Cormac McCarthy
- Watching *Game of Thrones*
- Running into Sunday morning megachurch traffic
- Talking politics
- Reading *Revelations* in the Bible

Things To Embrace

Micro-dosing on gratitude. Box breathing. Writing in a journal. Reading the *Psalms*, especially the psalms of lamentation. Mindfulness. The Jesus prayer. Walks after work. Sending funny memes to friends. Lifting weights. Getting lost in a local bookstore. Ironing shirts. Wordle. Shooting free throws in the driveway. Marco Polo-ing with my wife or Josh. Drinking water. Eating carrots. Being around people that make me laugh. Smiling. Slow Sunday mornings. Taking a long hot shower. One hour naps. U2 songs, especially from the Joshua Tree album. Sonic runs. Golfing. Saturday morning waffles with my son. Listening to a podcast episode of *Smartless*. Silencing my phone after 8 p.m. Sitting on the back porch. Attempting the Ted Lasso dance. Quoting Uncle Eddie lines from *Christmas Vacation*. Breaking in new shoes. Experiencing flow. Reading anything by Anne Lamott. Designing a new assessment for my students. Quiet and well-lit spaces. Helping a student with their writing. Writing a college recommendation. Lighting a candle. The month of October. 80s movies, especially *Say Anything*. Encouraging someone. Letting the call go to voicemail. Silence.

How To Show Up For Someone

So many people did me right during my darkest days of depression. Here's advice I would offer based on what I experienced by those who rallied around me.

- Know that when you just show up, you have provided us 99% of what we need.
- Put away your phone and listen.
- Two words of invitation. *Say more.*
- Avoid saying *pull it together* or *come on, cheer up* unless you are going to provide an instruction manual that makes a 100% guarantee.
- Grabbing coffee will work some time. But a walk is even better. Because then you both don't have to look at each other much. Which can actually be a really good thing, creating a safe space for your friend to open up without having to make eye contact.

- No Scripture—especially if you are a Calvnist. Double predestination and divine providentialism doesn't help. Unless that person is a TULIP Calvinist. Then have at it.

- Don't take it personally. Depressives like drunks will say and do things that aren't rational or intentional. Try to appreciate that it is an illness.

- Educate yourself. Ignorance only alienates. Understand that what you might think is easy to do—going to the mall or getting a pedicure, for example—might be a task too tall for a depressive.

- Meet them where they *are*. Not where they *ought* to be. Or where you hoped they would be. Ask how you can support them. Most of the time, simply showing up and being with them is enough.

- None of it is your fault. Be kind to yourself.

- Attempts at humor and levity are welcome. Laugher has curative power, even if it is short-term. A good meme or movie line or inside joke is usually a welcome escape, a nice little dopamine dab.

- Do the best you can not to alienate them any more than they already feel when they are around other normal, well-adjusted human beings. Trust me. They already feel like a bug or alien life form. If they show up with unmatched socks, just roll with it. Or wear a T-shirt with a big coffee stain on it; just treat it as art or a Rorschach test. If they ghost you for a few days, don't get mad or freak out. It's not you. If they suddenly suffer from a depressive type of Tourettes and "double fucks" you randomly, just nod and smile like they gave you a compliment. And if they cry over whether or not they should add oak milk to their Starbucks latte, just ignore their tears. That too shall pass. Do the best you can to normalize their abnormal behavior. The less they feel like you think they are a freak the better.

- When in doubt, say nothing. Error on the side of silence.
- If there is something you can take off their plate—do it. They will be so thankful. Most days, if there is even one piece of fruit on the plate, it is too much.
- Above all, be patient. It's all about playing the long game with us. Depression has an unnaturally natural ebb and flow to it, an undulating cadence, a timeline that isn't going to fit your timeline, a movement that can be maddening because of the many squiggles of emotional volatility, with progress forward, then regression backward, then more forward progress. Do the best you can to remain the flat line that runs through the squiggly line that is them. Your consistency matters.

↑
You

Telos And Logos

In college, I first read Victor Frankl's memoir *Man's Search for Meaning*. Frankl was a Holocaust survivor who endured the extreme version of a bad situation. The book is all about reframing perspective. The central question it poses is: *How can you be enmeshed in the absolute worst thing and have the power to reframe it to experience it differently?* The key to this perspective shift involves identifying and living into your *telos* and *logos*.

Telos is your goal, aim, or purpose. It's the target the arrow seeks to hit. *Logos* is your meaning, task, or assignment. It's the bullseye of the arrow's aim. As a psychotherapist, Frankl, drawing on his experience at Auschwitz, developed a seminal theory and practice called logotherapy. In logotherapy, you don't lie down on a couch and talk about yourself. Instead, you sit upright in a chair and listen to someone else talk to you. The focus isn't on your happiness, but on your suffering—not the pleasurable parts of life, but the painful ones.

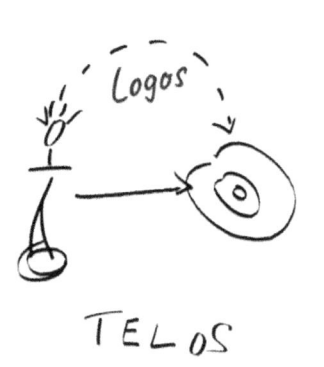

With a logotherapist, everything becomes an act of discernment—listening to your life and identifying the concrete assignment you are called to fulfill in your specific context of suffering. For Frankl, this meant writing his manuscript and caring for the sick patients in the concentration camp. For others, it might be surviving to see a spouse or child again. For still others, it could have been offering fellow inmates small, daily acts of kindness, like sharing a cigarette or an extra ladle of soup.

Frankl argued that to reframe our perspective, we must shift the question from *Why me?* to *What's my why?* This is never easy. In our natural field of vision, we see only negative energy charges. In Frankl and his inmates' case, this meant focusing on suffering, exhaustion, and unremitting acts of barbarity, cruelty, and dehumanization. Historians tell us that Frankl and others in concentration camps had a 1-in-28 chance of survival. Many inmates succumbed to what was known as *barbed wire syndrome*. After smoking their last cigarette, they would run into the barbed wire. The despair was palatable in the camps, as omnipresent as the smoke plumes rising above the crematorium furnaces.

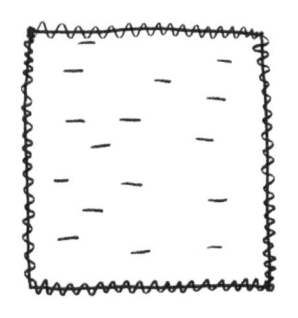

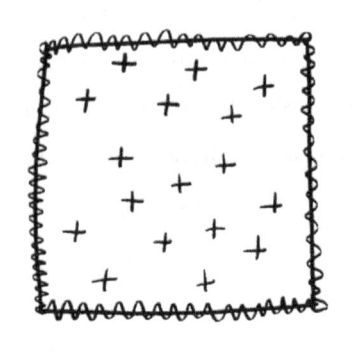

Frankl understood that sometimes we lack the freedom to change our external conditions. In those circumstances, our only choice is to change our inner attitude. Our freedom lies in the ability to take a stand toward the conditions we face. Only by making that inner choice can our field of vision change. What was once a matrix of negative charges can transform into an environment humming with positive charges of *telos* and *logos*.

Many days, I felt trapped inside a barbed-wire brain. Depression has a way of unspooling long cables of barbed wire around everything in the panorama of perception. All I could see were negative subatomic charges—a bleak, existential matrix devoid of *telos* and *logos*. The reality was this: I had embraced a victim narrative. I was playing the role of the lead victim, grossly misunderstood, tried-judged-and-executed in the court of public opinion. The entire clown show was a miscarriage of justice—a sham trial.

During one of my one-on-one sessions in Dallas, my counselor asked if I had ever heard of Frankl. I felt goosebumps. I nodded my head and smiled. That question catalyzed a series of conversations where my counselor invited me to sit up, stop talking, and start listening—really listening—for the *telos* and *logos* inside my pain and suffering.

Over time, something shifted. I began to see little swirling balls of atomic positive charges reappearing in the pupils of my eyes.

Frederick Nietzsche once wrote, *He who has a why to live for can bear almost any how.*

In the darkest moments, when I wanted to die, I thought of my family. My purpose was my people—a primal force as ancient as the earth.

They were my why.

My l*ogos*.

Getting well and staying well for them continues to be the animating *telos* of my life.

Reasons And Loves

My closest friend, Josh Banner, once told me: God has loves, not reasons.

That's always stuck with me—not just the beautiful theology but also the implicit anthropology. If we are created in the image of God, then we are what we love.

I'll say that last part again:

We are what we love.

And I'll add something else I also believe to be true:

We are what loves us.

We're all familiar with René Descartes's famous dictum: I think, therefore I am. My experiences tell me this is partially correct. I would argue that Brene Brown's seminal work confirms another truth I hold: the primary emotion we desire to experience is love. I am who I am because of whom I have loved, who has loved me, and what I have experienced as love.

Maybe the other half of Descartes' dictum is this: I love, therefore I am; and I am loved, therefore I am. We are the products of our loves. I wouldn't be alive today if it weren't for the loves of my life. I know that sounds cliche and drippy, something said during a Golden Globe or Emmy acceptance speech, but it's a truth I believe down to my bones.

Now. I could make a compelling list of reasons to stay alive. All good, sound, rational reasons why. Hypothetically, you and I might grab a cup of coffee, and I might say things like:

- You may feel a sense of cosmic and existential loneliness on this planet and in this galaxy, but you aren't alone. You're in a shadowland, but you're not isolated. This dark universe is populated by millions of people just like you.
- You want to stick your head in the oven and turn up the gas. You want to kill yourself. Well, the silver lining: things can't really get any worse. If you're living in rock bottom, the only direction is up.

- You struggle with self-hatred? Take a number and get in line. We're all self-centered slobs and beasts, but beneath the layers of fat and fur, there's something wonderfully human in each of us.
- You have a diagnosis, a label? Okay. I'm pretty sure if everyone saw a therapist or psychologist, they'd have a diagnosis and label too.
- Minds have their own weather circulation. Right now, you're in a super cell of tornadic activity. But super cells eventually run out of wind, rain, and energy. Hold on. A cool front with blue skies and sunshine is coming.

- The pain lies. Nothing lasts forever. Ignore it.

- Einstein's theory of relativity tells us that we're in a constant state of motion. Minds move. Personalities shift. Perspectives change relative to their environments and circumstances. Right now, your life is a total eclipse of darkness. The urge to end it all is at its apex. Don't do it. Remember, life is not still. Wait. You are moving through space and time, and eventually, you'll break through the darkness into a supernova of incandescent light and shining stars.
- The pain you feel now is part of the joy to come. You will dance again to a Taylor Swift song. You'll try something

scary but exhilarating, like THC gummies or karaoke. Life is out there, just waiting for you.
- You might be stuck in this rut for a while, but this one beautiful and strange world isn't going anywhere. Hang on by your fingernails if you can. Choosing life is always worth it in the end.

Any one of these reasons might do the trick. It's not that we aren't rational creatures that don't respond to compelling logic. I've just found that in really dark moments, I need something deeper—something that moves my mind into my heart. Something that connects me to the core of my being, reminding me of what makes me feel most alive in my skin and bones.

I need the trans-rationality of love.

And I've discovered that love isn't found in the universals but the particulars—at the molecular, cellular, and atomic level. It's a funky paradox, for sure. The smaller the thing, the more connected I feel to the larger reality—a larger reality that pulses, animates, and hums with the life force integrating all things into a whole that galaxies, solar systems, and universes can't even contain. Call it God, ultimate reality, the divine, the transcendent, the Oversoul, the grand mystery, the prime mover, the source of all things, the supreme being—language fails here. We enter the realm of negation, the apophatic, the indescribable.

I believe that in times of hopelessness and despair, what we need more than reasons to stay alive are loves. Specifically, love that surprises us— love that catches us off guard, makes our hearts skip a beat, and takes our breath away just long enough to remind us that breath itself is a gift.

In my lowest moments, I aspire to notice the loves grounded in the earthy tones and textures of daily life. I discipline myself to pay attention at the granular level of the mundane: the dappled things, the bibliosmia smell of old books; the playful, giddy mash-up of words in E.E. Cummings's poetry; walks around the school lake, the fall foliage, kids playing tag, and baby ducks in springtime.

And, of course, some of my all-time favorite loves: when my wife shimmies her shoulders before digging into chips and queso, bursts into spontaneous 1950s songs with her dad, or cracks an inside joke just for me, hermetically sealed for the rest of the world.

I am reminded of what has been set to song by many musicians, captured on canvas by so many artists, written into words by so many poets, and proclaimed as wisdom by so many philosophers and theologians:

The salvation of humanity is through love and in love.

In the end, I believe we are saved in and through each other—by the way we love and allow ourselves to be loved in this beautiful, messy world.

Things I Can Do Again That I Never Thought I Would

- 100 consecutive push ups.
- Smile spontaneously.
- Enjoy Oklahoma sunsets.
- Laugh until my abdomen aches.
- Fit into my 33W 32L pants.
- Hit my driver long and straight.
- Read an entire 600-page book like *Dune*.
- Go a whole day without a nap.
- Dance in the kitchen with my wife.
- Do 25 consecutive dips.
- Dream future dreams.
- Sub-create ex materia.
- Run a half marathon. (Just josh'in. To quote Roy Kent: "Fuck no!")
- Go to a public concert.
- Speak at public events.
- Say no to ice cream sandwiches.
- Say yes to salads, without gobs of ranch.
- Beat my son in ping pong (best out of five).
- Crack jokes.
- Coach basketball, even getting a technical foul for an explosive, expletive-riddled burst of passion for bad officating!

- Wear Lululemon workout shirts.
- Wake up at 6 a.m. excited for work.
- Post on social media (more discerningly).
- Enjoy running into my boss on campus, no lizard brain.
- Sing with the car windows down.
- Break 80 on the links.
- Host poker night.
- Organize and host the faculty/staff golf tournament.
- Vacation and not think once about work.
- Enjoy alone time in my own skin.

What A Healthy Enneagram 4 Does

- Embrace their magical purple unicorn-ness.
- Detach without withdrawing.
- Play team ball.
- Experience creative flow for days.
- Watch a rom-com, even one with Matthew McConaughey and Jennifer Lopez.
- At the very least, toe-taps to a Taylor Swift song.
- Celebrate others' talents without green-eyed dragon envy.
- Doesn't avoid conflict. Shows a spine.
- Pick their spots and times to emote with high intensity.
- Text people back the same day.
- Finish what they start.

Things I Give Myself Permission To Say Now (That I Didn't Before)

- No.
- Not today.
- Interesting. I see things differently.
- I need you to listen.
- I need some space.
- No, I am not okay.
- I won't let you shame me.
- I am worthy of love.
- I won't let you gaslight me.
- I fucked up, and I am sorry.
- Can I have a redo?
- I need mercy.
- I am forgiven.
- I am enough.

The Hero's Journey—Homecoming

The hero's journey ends when the protagonist returns home with a boon.

The gift is not an object, something made of materials.

The gift is the rebirth and transformation of the person's consciousness and character. He or she returns to the community different, grown up, evolved, more mature. There's been a sort of alchemy of personal transformation—from the metal of hubris to the gold of humility, from the metal of knowledge to the gold of wisdom, from the metal of self-centeredness to the gold of others-centeredness.

When I look back on my own hero's journey, I see that the gross metal of my humanity was transformed in the fire of the abyss. At the time, the abyss was a fucking nightmare. I would never want to experience that kind of pain, suffering, and trauma again.

And…

Looking back, I see how the abyss was a blessing inside the curse. It's true. While I don't ever want to live through all that shitshow trauma again, I also somehow can't imagine living without it. It's a perplexing paradox. Another fucking annoying mystery.

Gifts

When I reach down and run my fingers through the dark dirt of past painful days, I discover gifts of grace buried in the hard soil of my suffering days.

Gifts that continue to heal my trauma and restore me to good health.

And, hopefully, gifts that are a balm to others in their suffering.

The Gift Of Gratitude

Depression has a way of blocking the arteries that releases gratitude through our bodies. Our thoughts become clouded by worry, anxiety, and sadness. As this happens, our feelings get sucked up into this dark and stormy weather system. We get caught in this circular vortex of negative thoughts and emotions, all of which makes depression and our outlook on life worse. Our lens of perspective on reality becomes discolored and cripples our ability to experience any kind of positive emotion.

The way we clean the lens of perspective is to practice gratitude. Dr. Phil Stutz calls this the Grateful Flow exercise. It only takes 30 seconds, and it's something all of us can practice, especially when we feel a dark cloud form over our thoughts and emotions. It's as simple as practicing these three simple steps:

- Close your eyes.
- Take two or three box breaths. Inhale for a count of four. Hold for a count of four. Exhale for a count of four.
- Now think of 4 to 5 things you're grateful for. Focus on simple, concrete things right inside your orbit of conscious

thought. Say what you are grateful for in a slow cadence, out loud. Let your teeth, mouth, and lips feel each word.

- I am grateful for my breath.
- I am grateful for my body that breathes these breaths.
- I'm grateful for this hot cup of coffee in my hand.
- I'm grateful for the crisp wind on my bare feet.
- I'm grateful for my dog nuzzled up against me.

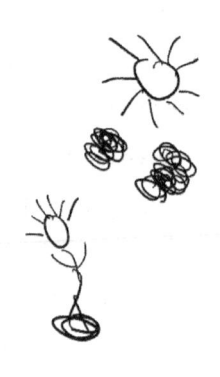

What you will find is that when you start with something simple and concrete, it is not long before you move from effortful cognition to a kind of effortless flow state. That's when you begin to feel the gratefulness circulating in and around and through your heart. As this happens, you will want to try to stay still enough to let the energy force eddy and flow in and around and through you to carry you upward. Often, my chest will soften. My body will relax. And the dark clouds will part, and I will feel the presence of something deliciously numinous melt away the depression. In that moment, I will simply try to surrender control to this light, warmth, and energy. I will try not to understand it in the rational mind, but to give in, opening myself up in my heart and soul to letting this trans-rational and mysterious, otherworldly presence give me what I need, graciously receiving the gift.

Gratitude is a discipline. It's a willful act, one that requires intention, attention, and repetition. Gratitude is not something you master, like chess or karate. Gratitude requires what Thomas Merton called a beginner's mindset. Each day we say to ourselves, *Let us begin again.* Today, I will try once again to show and express and speak gratitude into the air, ecosystem, and universe that I inhabit.

My best friend Josh and I send Marco Polo messages to each other, if not daily, then regularly. We always begin our Marcos with a declaration of gratitude. It's become a kind of liturgical act, a way in which each of us does the work of attending to, paying attention to, and rehearsing what specifically in our days and in our lives we have experienced to give thanks for. There is real power when Josh and I speak of that which we are grateful for. It's as though we are bearing witness to each other's life and the mysterious, beautiful, and fragile gift that it is.

The Gift Of Prayer

On the last day of the program, I received my diploma—a laminated mini-card with the Serenity Prayer on it.

God, grant me the serenity to accept things I cannot change,
the courage to change the things I can,
and the wisdom to know the difference.

Many people who suffer from addiction know this prayer. It's the cornerstone of AA's 12 steps and traditions to recovery. To this day, I carry around my little laminated Serenity Prayer card in my wallet. Sometimes, I will take it out of my wallet, run my fingers over the plastic edges, and read the prayer to myself, remembering where I once was, where I am now, and giving thanks. So much of prayer is remembering.

It's a funny thing. The older I get, the simpler things get. Prayer is no different.

My prayers now are more Serenity Prayer-ish. More Psalm 23 than Psalm 119. More Hemingway than Dostoevsky. Short, terse, economical. Jesus himself seemed to subscribe to this school of prayer. He told his students essentially something to the effect of, "Get to your point. God has good hearing, better than a wax moth."

Most days, I pray one prayer. It's an orthodox prayer, ancient and eastern. It's called the Jesus Prayer. The Jesus Prayer is rooted in scripture, specifically taken from accounts in the gospels that involve encounters between Jesus and a blind man, ten lepers, and a tax collector. What connects all three characters is the mutual sense of desperation. Jesus met all of them right where they were—in their pain, confusion, and fucked-upness— and showed them mercy: the healing, inclusive, and generous kind of mercy.

You would think I first heard of the Jesus Prayer in the place where people talk a lot about Jesus—church. You'd be wrong. I actually first heard of the Jesus Prayer in J.D. Salinger's little novel *Franny and Zooey*. The main character, Franny, is a twentysomething woman, from upper Manhattan—sophisticated, modern, rich, the kind of character that would run around with Serena and Blaire on *Gossip Girl*. Franny shares the same disenchantment and cynicism of the times. She feels hollow, bored, dirtied by institutional forces marked by avarice and powerlust. In desperation, Franny turns to the Jesus Prayer. She teaches it to Zooey, and they pray the ancient prayer while lying in an expensive bathtub, dressed in fur coats, in between drags of a cigarette and sips of gin.

Traditionally, the Jesus Prayer is made up of seven words:

Lord Jesus Christ, have mercy on me.

In the monastic tradition, the Jesus Prayer is referred to as an arrow prayer. Arrow prayers are short prayers that only take a few seconds to pray—they are shot up to God, aimed to penetrate darkness or fear and direct our thoughts quickly to the divine.

When I pray the Jesus Prayer, I like to hold prayer beads. I'm a tactile being, so I like something to touch and roll around and fidget with. My aim with the Jesus Prayer is simple: to pray the prayer as often as I can. Or at least as often as I can remember to. Because God knows, I need all the help I can get to save me from myself and my natural proclivity to fuck things up.

Here's the thing.

I believe we are all fundamentally religious beings.

When I say religious, I'm not talking about creeds, dogmas, codified beliefs, superstitions, rituals, traditions, or secret societies. I'm talking about religion in the original and radical sense of the word. At its etymological root, religion comes from the Latin word *ligio* which is translated as something that binds, connects, and holds together. *Ligio* is where we get the word for ligament. Think about that for a second. What does a ligament do but hold bone, tissue, and muscles all together. Without ligaments, our flesh, bone, and skeletons collapse. When religion is at its best, it operates as the force and energy that holds everything together in the universe, including you and me, your barista, nail specialist, state senator, and miniature schnauzer.

I don't know about you, but there are many days where I feel like I'm going to rip apart at the seams—all 185 pounds of my flesh, blood, water, and bone disintegrating until I'm nothing but carbon, calcium, and potassium elements, broken all the way down into flakes in an ashtray on a motorcycle.

It's the line from Y.B. Yeats's apocalyptic poem: *The center can not hold*. That's me most days. On the verge of crashing down like a Jenga tower. That's where the Jesus Prayer comes in for me. And I'm only speaking for myself. The Jesus Prayer helps center me, drawing me into that confessional space—what German theologian Deitrich Bonhoeffer referred to as religionless religion—translation: the no-bullshit zone of costly grace that comes with making ourselves nakedly known in our fullfuckedupness.

The Jesus Prayer helps me crawl down into my heart.

The Jesus Prayer keeps me grounded, humble, earthy, dirty-cloddy.

The Jesus Prayer helps me connect to something larger, transcendent, numinous-smelling, otherworldly, and spiritual.

Most importantly, the Jesus Prayer reminds me that we all need mercy, and when I say all, I mean all—*including those who wear MAGA hats and get excited to see what Kim Kardashian wore to the Met Gala.* Wink.

As we close this chapter, it is only fitting that I offer up for all of us the prayer that down through centuries has offered hope, comfort, and light to people of every stripe and color, political party, and breed of dog owner.

Lord Jesus Christ, have mercy on us all.

The Gift Of Presence

In therapy, I have learned a lot about the root system beneath depression and anxiety. At its base, depression is about our past, while anxiety is about our future. Both represent something in space and time that are beyond our control. And both represent something in space and time that often takes control of us.

What depression and anxiety share in common is the psychic power to pull us out of the circular flow of the present. Part of what healing from trauma does is allow us to be more present in the present—in our bodies, and in our hands, arms, legs, and toes. All our embodied energies flowing in the direction of the other's embodied presence.

During my depressed state, I can't tell you how many times my wife would shut down in a conversation with me.

"Josh, what did I just say?"

Silence. Wracking my short-term memory.

"Exactly. You have that glazed-over look again."

"I promise I'm listening."

"You might be hearing me, but you aren't listening to me."

"I am." (Lie.)
"No, you are always somewhere else."

It's a strange phenomenon how our body can be in one place in space and time, and our mind is in an entirely different space and time—sometimes even in multiple spaces and places simultaneously. It's a real *Star Trek*-y sci-fi mindfuck. I can be sitting at the kitchen table with my wife, listening to her talk about her workday, while simultaneously transporting back to my boss's office, rehashing a conversation with him, or taking a phone call with an angry parent. I am here and not here, in my body and outside my body, present and absent.

Part of what healed trauma has done is allow me to be where my feet are, more fully present in the present. When I am with my son at breakfast, or my wife at dinner, or a student in my office, I find that I can concentrate and stay right there in the moment. Which means that I'm more in my prefrontal cortex—the part of my brain that works as an air traffic control for sensory input, helping me regulate the white noise.

I'm not perfectly present. I still have moments where my wife will snap her fingers and say, "Clock in, Bottomly!" I still sometimes get stuck in the space between my ears, like an elevator shaft.

We're all forever in a state of perpetual evolution. I'm no different. And like everyone else, I'm learning and growing in the skill of practicing the presence of people. And for that, I am grateful for a gift that never stops giving—like Clark W. Griswold's jelly-of-the-month-club bonus.

The Gift Of Joy

Not long ago, I was sitting with two colleagues at an oyster bar in St. Louis. One colleague was an administrator at a private school in Kansas City. The other colleague worked at a peer school in Oklahoma City. We were catching up and shooting the shit. At one point, one of them said in an unguarded, quasi-inebriated state, "Where did the joy of the job go?"

Veritas in utrem.

We sat in silence together.
Nothing needed to be said.

Helicopter and submarine and
lawnmower parents, and

grade-obsessed and hyper-
anxious and perfectionistic kids, and

college admission pressures, and

meddling Board of Trustees, and

the standardization of curriculum (aka teaching to the test), and

utilitarian product-driven consumeristic education models, and

data-driven administrators, and

longer days, and

shorter summers, and

pandemics, and

political polarization, and

rampant student absenteeism, and

artificial intelligence, and

the whole arms race to stay competitive in the market.

As I listened to my friends in between oysters, I couldn't help but empathize with their frustrations in the ever-changing world of education. I knew firsthand everything they were describing; their pathos was real, and something that had sunk its vampire fangs into my neck veins too, sucking the very life force out of me. The difference was that I had discovered, by sheer grace, an antidote that had cured me in such a way that I had recovered my sense of joy.

Here's the hard-fought truth that I've discovered about joy. Perhaps you will resonate with this as well.

At its essence, joy is a deep-down aliveness that reverberates in our whole body.

Notably, joy happens at the dynamic intersection of our heart's deepest gladness and the world's greatest need.

For me, that joyful criss-cross of gladness and need involves helping kids find their yawp.

Life is full of never-ending "and's." No getting around this conjunction. But I believe that joy is not found in the abdication or absence of the and's but in the thick maw and mess of all the and's. I believe it all comes back to our sense of vocation—one's calling. There are certainly things in life we have to do. And there are things we can do. Even things we want to do but can't. But there are also things that we need to do because the world needs them done, and no one else can do those things like you can do them. That's where the joy is, where our special somebodiness does something in this world that bears witness to our special, unique, and holy gift. For me, the last place I need to be—and that the world needs me to be—is in an office behind a desk, looking at reports, populating spreadsheets, managing adults, and meeting with irate parents. Somebody else is uniquely made for that vocational groove. For me, the fizz in the Coke is when I am with kids 173 days a year—guiding, coaching, inspiring, explaining, listening, modeling, discerning, asking questions, drawing doodles, playing games, laughing, sympathizing, empathizing, disciplining, advocating, cheering on, and loving, regardless if they bring their A-game, B-game, C-game, D-game, or F game.

So, it harkens back to the question: What is your yawp?

What is it that makes you feel deep-down aliveness in your wholebody?

What is that golden intersection between the y-axis of your heart's gladness and the x-axis of the world's need around you?

Lean in and listen for the answer to these questions.

For therein lies the key to rediscovering joy.
I truly believe this.

More than ever.

The Gift Of Bad Days

I still have bad days. I am human, after all, living in this dark, strange, fucked-up modern world. Like everyone else, I'll wake up with a doomsday hangover from something I read online the night before. Or sit up and feel my almost-50-something body groan with knotted pain in my lower back.

I'll have mornings where I'll forget to take my meds and walk through the day with zombiebrain, only to wake up in the middle of the next night drenched in sweat and scared shitless from a dream I had of a grizzly bear chasing me in a hotel staircase crowded by people who won't fucking move.

I'll have moments, where out of nowhere, my body will suffer an earthquake—3.6 on the magnitude scale. My hands will shake, and I'll struggle for breath like I'm under water, almost blacking out.

I'll have intrusive thoughts, panicky ones, where I'm sure I'm going to have a brain aneurysm; dark thoughts, as well, where I hear a bullet go through my brain and all goes black silence, except the sound of a fly buzzing on the windowpane.

My wife will sometimes catch me with that vacuous look in my eye, physically there in body, but floating in the ether of my mind. Even my son, on occasion, will look in my face and see sadness or anxiety in my eyes, and ask me if I'm okay. I'll fake a smile and lie. A son shouldn't have to do mental health checks with his dad. It should be the other way around.

On bad days, I try to remember that this too will pass. In those troubling moments, I make a conscious effort to zoom out to a 20,000-foot level in hopes of recover a more expansive viewpoint that sees the contours of the whole human experience—a landscape that undulates with peaks and valleys and contains endless circular movements and experiences of eucatastrophe.

Eventually, the day ends, and I'll give thanks that I survived the storm. I'll turn off the lights and try to give my body eight hours of sleep that night so that I can wake up with renewed energy.

If anything, bad days help us savor the good days, like a cherry Lifesaver in a pack full of lemon ones. And the bad days remind us that most of the people that we live with, work with, pass in the Starbucks line, and see in our social media feeds are secretly carrying a heavy burden and are just trying to do the best they can to hold up the sky, in hopes that a shitton of wind, rain, and hail doesn't break loose, sending them in search of an umbrella and dry socks.

The Gift Of Place

A towering oak tree sprawls near the campus lake.

The tree feels old, ancient.

Some of her branches reach out for forty feet and then bend down to touch the ground.

I often sit under her shade in silence.

Looking through her thick, veiny branches, I can see the sky in a hundred little blue jigsaw pieces.

The tree speaks to me.

Of place and space.

Of rootedness and fruitfulness.

And, after twenty years in this community, I realize that this place is not perfect, nor will it ever be.

But it is good.

And for that I am deeply grateful.

Selah

"The divine hears our one-worded prayers," writes Anne Lamott.

Wow.

Things That Fill Me With Wow Again

Oklahoma sunrises. The choir of cicadas chirring in the evening dusk. The jumpupgreetings and happypaws of my dog. The words and stories of Colson Whitehead and Toni Morrison. Wind chiming through the Bradford pear trees. Blooming crepe myrtles in the spring. Hummingbirds in flight. A hardcover book filled with pulpy wood pages between my curious fingers. Listening to my son make music in his bedroom. The prose of Cole Arthur Riley. The photography of Dawoud Bey. The poetry of Mary Oliver. Steve Martin and Martin Short's comedic synergy—they still got it! *The Invitation* podcast. Laughing with my wife all these years later when we watch *Just Friends*. Playing Uno with my advisees on Wednesdays. Listening to my students discuss literature. Sunday afternoon naps. My mom's faith in the face of cancer. My dad's love for my mom in the face of her cancer battle. The first day of school. The last day of school. Christmas. Easter. The Resurrection Man.

The Brain And Body—Part Four

I said it earlier, unabashedly: I am a meds person. I own that. I rely on big pharma to provide me medication to keep me balanced and level and out of my zombie-apocalyptic brain. I give thanks every morning as I palm my red and white pills and gulp them down with water. That said, I am also fully aware that my health and well-being cannot rely solely on medication. The antidepressants that work their way through my brain and body are only as effective as they relate to my healthy habits and behaviors. My mental health is not a solo act. It is an ensemble. A choreographed dance. Nothing works alone. Nothing harmonizes in isolation. That's the point. And that's the fallacy we're always fighting against in our modern, individualistic culture. We've swallowed the placebo of post-Enlightenment nihilism that promulgates a set of binaries and reductions to our detriment, divorcing our minds from our bodies, and reducing our humanity to a bunch of bogus nothing-buts — nothing-but-chemicals, nothing-but-animal-instincts, nothing-but-electrical signals, nothing-but-neurosis, nothing-but-subconscious-desires, and nothing-but-environmental stimuli. This kind of reductionistic apparatus has caused us to treat symptoms but not root causes. We create a cure that preserves the disease.

At a basic phenomenological level, we all know that reducing everything to a matter of matter just doesn't work in reality. Our human experience deconstructs such overly simplistic thinking under the guise of bourgeoisie sophistication. Our mental health requires an integrative project, a coordinated effort in mind, body, and spirit. I point to Dr. Stutz's Life Force Pyramid. His pyramid consists of three levels—the body, relationships, and yourself. At each level, Stutz fleshes out how we must treat our body and nurture relationships and care for self. Notably, Stutz is not a dualist, nor a reductionist. He practices holism, a non-dual way of thinking, one that integrates spirituality into his practice and treatment of patients. If I amend and personalize Stutz's pyramid, I would draw a dotted line through all three levels to illustrate the fact that medication runs through all of them in an integral way in me.

In my paradigm, it works like this:

It is meds + body—racquetball at the YMCA, dumbbell presses, park walks, 6-irons, and REM sleep cycles.

It is meds + others—hugs, cuddles, feet touches, hangouts, the water cooler.

It is meds + self—self-mercy, self-grace, self-effacing laughter, self-care, and self-love.

And if I were to add one extra all-encompassing level, it would be meds + faith—centering prayer, lectio divina, serving others, and practicing gratefulness.

Experience has taught me that the day I cease to integrate all of these different levels and sublevels into my daily cocktail of medication is the day I begin to dis-integrate in mind, body, and spirit.

It either all holds together, or it all collapses, like the Death Star.

Fruit

Next week, I will attend the 3rd annual Exposition of Learning at my school. This is the alternative final exam for the American Design course—the 11th-grade, team-taught, project-based interdisciplinary course that my school launched strategically three years ago. For almost a decade, our humanities department had dreamed of offering this course, and now, all these years later, it is a living, breathing, animating reality on our school's campus. Seeing a dream become a real thing is about the coolest thing I have ever experienced professionally. And even though I no longer have any official involvement with the school's most innovative program, I get the unique pleasure of bearing witness to the gift and vitality of this course and program. Next Tuesday, I will sit among a packed audience in the theater and get to hear four different presentations by 11th-grade students on city-wide design challenges that focus on an Oklahoma City-centered issue related to the family, the environment, health care, and education. Each team will walk us through their journey of partnering with a local non-profit organization, using human-centered design thinking to solve a problem. This is transformative education—the kind of real-world, hands-on, authentic learning that all kids need, not just for the mid-twenty second-century skills, but to offer our students a real taste of how they can be architects of repair in their cities and communities.

Till the soil and spread the seed into the fallow ground, rake the seed into the dark soil, water it, and nurture it with care and love through each stage of photosynthesis, and watch and bear witness to what will emerge over time, through seasons and cycles and patience—something like fruit that will feed gurglystomachs for generations to come.

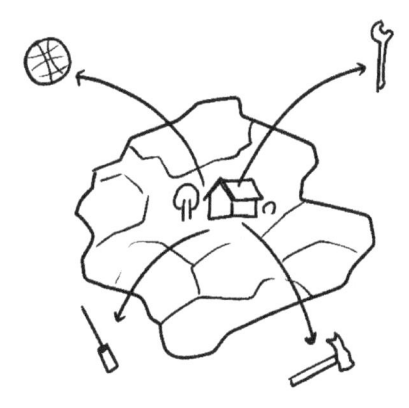

Existence And Paradox

Being human is hard AF. It's not that difficult to look around and see the kind of cruelty and meanness that will take your breath away and make you want to move to Nova Scotia or Zihuantanejo. Some days, we don't want to get out of bed. We'd prefer to stay in our sweats and wool socks; the world has already won. The modern antidote for the barking madness seems to be two-pronged—busyness and plugged-in-ness. How often will I ask someone, "How are you?" and their immediate response, with a dramatic tinge of exhaustion will be, "Good, so so busy." I'm guilty of this same canned response, feeling compelled to say it as though busyness represents some kind of shiny badge of adult status. Busyness is the drug of choice in our hyperactive culture—whether with the constant hustle and grind of work, kids' soccer tournaments, Orange Theory workouts, fantasy football draft nights, life group get-togethers, or theme parties at the neighborhood pool house. We numb ourselves by staying in constant motion, like an overbalanced wheel. The other modern antidote appears to be the rapidly evolving, expanding, ubiquitous presence of the virtual world. Watching kids today, they seem perfectly content as human avatars, wired in 24-7, living in a pixelated cyber-reality—endlessly scrolling, liking, selfie-ing, augmenting, emoji-ing, photoshopping, texting, sexting, shopping, gambling, gaming, binging, multitasking, multiversing. While I am certainly not immune to the bright allure of the cyber universe, I also find that I can not float around in the ether of the virtual world too long before I feel the need to reconnect with my body, like someone returning to the surface for oxygen after holding their breath for a long time underwater.

I can fully understand why people are quick to pull the lever that opens up the trap door, offering them an escape from embodiment and interiority. Because we know that if we feel things and think hard enough and long enough about things, eventually we will have to feel and think about the stuff we don't really want to feel or think about—our ragged mortality, saggy neck skin, bunioned big toes—all of which will inevitably get shoveled over by dirt, fertilizer, and earthworms.

It's just a fact of life that no matter how much Ozempic we inject into our bodies, or Botox we put into our faces, or silicone gel we squeeze into our breasts, we will grow old and jiggly, see our butts in the mirror and cry, turn curmudgeonly, eventually get sicky sick, and finally stop breathing altogether.

None of us are getting out of life alive.

If that isn't macabre enough for you, there is the inevitable fact that everyone we love and care for on this silent planet—including our Amazon driver, favorite royal member, and family parakeet—will also stop breathing and die. This morbid thought alone can make us depressed and anxious and reach for an ice cream sandwich. But it is also a gift. A gift because we are the only species that knows this and thinks about this inevitable reality. Depression, in this vein, makes us a truly remarkable species—one that has imagined, dreamed up, and created remarkable things.

Remarkable Created Things:

Fire, words, languages, rituals, rites of passage, symbols, civilizations, stories, art, books, dance, love songs, sex positions, origami, cashmere sweaters, Lululemon leggings, Apple products, *Netflix*, Pikes Peak, Pacific Ocean, 3D-printers, Hallmark Christmas movies, Mike Tyson's *Punch Out*, Southwest airlines—and two free bags, the Beatles, Daisy Jones & the Six, Shakespeare plays, Batman's cave, Peter Parker's secret as Spider-Man, Steve Urkel, E.T., Dave Eggers's *A Heartbreaking Work of a Staggering Genius*, Jerry Goldsmith's theme song for *Hoosiers*, Chicago deep dish pizza, Wrigley Field, PS5s, *Minecraft*, Dairy Queen blizzards, Vincent Van Gogh's "Starry Night," Arnold Palmers, Outback's mac and cheese, Egyptian pyramids, Notre Dame Cathedral, Burj Khalifa, Louvre Museum, The Sphere in Las Vegas, Hollywood sign, the 1980s by John Hughes, perms, mullets, denim jeans, light sabers, the Golden Gate bridge, Great Wall of China, Pebble Beach's 18th hole, Amen Corner, escape rooms, line dances, Vladimirov's "Thunderbolt" chess move, Simone Biles's double layout with a half-twist, *Garage Band*, boy bands—especially The New Kids on the Block, *Pac-Man*, Megan Rapino's cross to Abby Wamback for the header goal, Kobe-to-Shaq for the alleyoop, Kareem's sky hook, Google's Waymo self-driving cars, *Jurassic Park*, Christmas Eve at the Griswolds, Kosmo Kramer, Kelly Clarkson, Elvis, Oprah, Beyonce, Phoebe, Chandler Bing, MJ's fadeaway, Magic's no-look pass, Kelly Kapowski and Zack Morris, Tom Haverford and Andy Dwyer, Homer and Marge Simpson, Wall-E and Eve, Buzz and Woody, Elsa and Anna, Belle and the Beast, Sonny and Cher—and the meteoric rise of bell bottoms, the imagination of George Lucas, the jazz of John Coltrain, the musical genius of Jon Batiste, the sermons of Dr. King, the voiceovers of Daniel Stern for *The Wonder Years*, the vocal range of Whitney Houston, the dance moves of Justin Timberlake, the television creations of Michael Schrur, the stand-up comedy of Dave Chapelle, the fiction of Toni Morrison, the political satire of Noah Trevor, the political sanity of Jon Stewart, the prose of Maya Angelou, the poetry of Billy Collins, the lyrical genius of Taylor Swift, the nefarious chemistry between Walter White and Jesse Pinkman in *Breaking Bad*, the floating Hallelujah Mountains of Pandora, the chocolate factory of Willy Wonka, Harry Potter and Hogwarts, Ents and eagles and elves of Middle-earth, *Marvel* universe, World Cup, Olympics, March Madness, Super Bowl commercials, Broadway musicals like *Wicked* and *The Lion King,* Lin-Manuel Miranda in *Hamilton*, Julia Andrews in *The Sound of Music*, Morgan Freeman as "Red" in *The Shawshank Redemption*, Val Kilmer as Doc Holiday in *Tombstone*, Rory and Lorelai in *Gilmore Girls*, Ross and Rachel in *Friends*, Coach Taylor and Tami Taylor in the TV hit-show *Friday Night Lights*, homecoming parades, prom night, podcasts, ChatGPT,

Birkenstocks, Crocs, retro Jordans, rubik cubes, John Neismith's rules of basketball, fly fishing, frisbee golf, Christmas lights, Festivus-for-the-rest-of-us, snow days and no school, snowball fights, snow angels, water balloon wars, pillow fights, Halloween candy, smores at a campfire, Captain Crunch, Golden Gooses, puppies, babies.

Chiaroscuro

During one of the COVID years, a history teacher quit (or retired early) mid-year, so I ran triage and taught 9th grade World History—something I'd never done before. During our study of the Renaissance, we all (including myself) learned about chiaroscuro, an art form that involves contrasting light and shade. In Correggio's painting entitled *The Holy Night*, for example, dark shadow was used to accentuate the light bathing baby Jesus in the arms of mother Mary. Correggio's painting captures the dialectic tension—the strange and mysterious fact that life and death live in jagged tension with each other, and that inevitably, the child will become a man who will become an outcast, who will become a criminal nailed a on a cross, and, based on what you believe, will become a Resurrection Man. Everyone and everything inevitably must go through the cycle of growth, evolution, entropy, calamity and death that leads to the good, the beautiful, the lovely, and the eternal. There is a eucatastrophic shape to the contours of the universe—a good calamity paradox at the heart of human existence. I can't explain this, but I can't explain it away. It's something I believe down in my bones, and, indefatigably, my life bears witness to this reality. Nevertheless, I still struggle daily to surrender to the eucatastrophic mystery that is baked into the whole thing. To live paradoxically requires a Kierkegaardian-like leap of faith—a willingness to become like a child again, a child who in his or her wildest imaginations, dreams of the fairy tale ending beyond the dragons, ringwraiths, and necromancers where everything tragic, ugly, and sad comes untrue.

Practice Resurrection

Seasons and natural rhythms have always fascinated me. My favorite season is fall, especially the month of October. Everything once green is now a patchwork quilt of vibrant colors—pumpkin oranges, cranberry reds, mulberry purples, and canary yellows. In the autumn, in many parts of the world, the leaves drop from the tree branches and the plants die. They turn brown, wither up, and lose their life. They remain this way for the winter—dormant, dead, lifeless, devoid of vitality. And then spring comes, and they burst into life again. Everything grows and sprouts and blooms, producing new leaves, leafy buds, and green shoots. For there to be spring, there has to be a fall and then a winter. For nature to spring to life, it first has to die. Death, then resurrection. Always in this order. Always in this cyclical rhythm. We see this same pattern at a cellular level. Our bodies are made up of trillions and trillions of tiny cells—37 trillion to be exact. Every day, 500 million of our cells die and regenerate through a process called cell regeneration. That means that about every seven years, we will literally grow a whole new body. Death gives way to life.

Right now, my 10th-grade students are in the final chapters of Dickens's *A Tale of Two Cities*. They are at the climactic part of the story where Charles Darnay awaits the guillotine for treason. On the eve of Darnay's execution, Sydney Carton weighs a fateful decision. Up to this point, Carton has played the role of the sad fatalist, prone to self-loathing and drunkenness. But as he walks the streets of Paris in the dead of night, Carton feels a flame growing firm within him, something recalling him to life. In the quiet shadows under the ominous street lights, Carton begins to recite Jesus' words: *I am the resurrection and the life, saith the Lord: he that believeth in me, though he were dead, yet shall he live.* This will be Sydney Carton's Gethsemane moment. The next day, Carton will hatch his secret plan. As a look-alike to Darnay, Carton will sneak Darnay out of the prison and take his place on the chopping block. For Sydney Carton, this final act of self-giving love, dying sacrificially in the place of another, derives its potency from his deep-down conviction beyond all hope that even though death gets the first word, it doesn't get the last word. Death will mysteriously lead to life. And that what happened in the middle of history to one ResurrectionMan will happen at the end of history for all people, including Sydney Carton. There will be an ultimate and final eucatastrophe. A resurrectionhumanity.

Here's what I believe:

Resurrection is not heaven. It's not up there. Or otherworldly.

Resurrection is earthy, fleshy, down here, this worldly, baked into the whole thing—seasons and rhythms and ecosystems and food chains and human bodies.

Resurrection isn't just something we hope for in the future. It's something we experience in the present, in the here-and-now.

American poet Wendell Berry famously wrote in one of his poems "Practice resurrection."

Practice resurrection.

Our cells and bodies practice resurrection every day.

Every time we sleep, wake up, and get up, we practice resurrection.

Every time we take deep breaths, inhale and exhale, we practice resurrection.

Every time we show up for someone in a dark place, we practice resurrection.

Every time we make someone feel seen, visible, heard, and loved, we practice resurrection.

Every time we begin again—with breathing and praying and listening and exercising and eating well and being grateful—we practice resurrection.

Every day we say "No" to killing ourselves and "Yes" to surviving today, and only today, we practice resurrection.

Anniversary Day

The three-year anniversary of my mental health recovery comes and goes like a mountain rain shower. By grace and grit, medication and therapy, prayer and exercise, and family and friends, I have come full circle; the hero's journey is now complete.

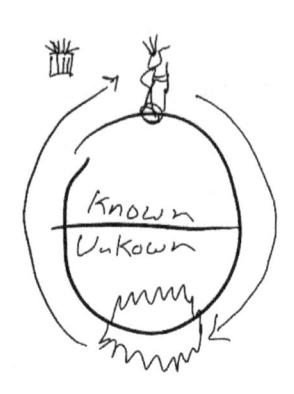

Today, I am back in the Shire, which for me has always been teaching. Thanks to the generosity of my boss, I have been given a new lease on life. I am back in the classroom where I belong. It's my little hobbit hole—that place I return to daily where I experience the simple joy of learning with and from my students. In ordinary moments, whether listening to my students engaged in a Harkness discussion, helping a student with a draft of a paper, or building a college list for one of my advisors, I feel that I have come all the way back.

The center somehow held.

Three years ago, I never would have imagined any of this possible. I thought by this point, I'd be ashes spread out near the garden rosebush or making wicker baskets in a facility somewhere in Oregon.

During my off hours now, I often take long walks around the lake that outlines the school. Some days I walk to remember. Other days, to forget. Most days, I walk to feel health and wellness circulate through my body and brain again. On this particular autumn morning, the cloudless sky is pearly blue, like water, deep and still. The air feels crisp and delicious on my hands and face. Tiny whorls of wind chime through the plum-colored foliage. As I watch the sun shimmer off the water's surface, I recall Dr. King's words spoken days before his assisination.

The end is reconciliation;
the end is redemption;
the end is the creation of the beloved community.

As I recall these words, I feel a renewed sense of gratitude and love for everyone and everything that lives and breathes and moves inside of my relational ecosystem. More than anything, I feel hope that even though calamity is baked into the whole thing called life, something else is baked into it too—something deeper, higher, more expansive, an unstoppable force that hums and beats and pulsates through the green shoots and leafy branches and fleshy veins of all things—an unconquerable good.

For in the end,

if we lean into the silence and

listen to our own breathing and

listen to our own beating heart and

listen to our own sacred bodies and

listen our own embodied souls,

we will hear what life is in all its strange and beautiful mystery.

A good calamity.

If you or someone you know is struggling with mental health or in crisis, help is available.

Call or text 988 or chat 988lifeline.org

Acknowledgement

A quest is a collaborative effort. This one was no different. I have a handful of people to thank for helping me fulfill my literary quest.

To Josh: You were at ground zero in a Chicago coffee shop to bear witness to the first incarnation of this manuscript.

To Whitney, Stephanie, and Sandy: Your honest, meticulous, and thoughtful feedback on my first major draft provided me with the encouragement I needed to go further up and further in with courage and vulnerability.

To Meera: Thank you for capturing my vision for the book cover through your artistic gift.

To Hezron, Jake, and the whole team that partnered with Telos Books: Your guidance, expertise, and support were invaluable during the latter stages of the publishing process.

To my son: You are my "Phial of Galadriel"—a source of light when all other lights have gone out.

And, finally, to my wife: You are my "Arwen"—my elf queen.